THE
GOSPEL
in the
PASSOVER

The Staff of Chosen People Ministries

Edited by Darrell L. Bock and Mitch Glaser

CHOSEN PEOPLE
MINISTRIES

241 East 51st Street
New York, NY 10022
Toll-free: 1-888-2-YESHUA

www.chosenpeople.com
www.messiahinthepassover.com

The Gospel in the Passover

© 2017 Chosen People Ministries

Published by Chosen People Ministries
241 E. 51st Street, New York, NY 10022

All Scripture quotations are taken from the *New American Standard Bible*® (NASB), © 1960, 1962, 1963, 1968, 1971, 1972, 1973, 1975, 1977, 1995 by The Lockman Foundation. Used by permission. www.Lockman.org.

Library of Congress Cataloging-in-Publication Data

ISBN 978-1-882675-25-8

Printed in the United States of America

17 18 19 20 21 / 5 4 3 2 1

THE GOSPEL IN THE PASSOVER

Clean out the old leaven so that you may be a new lump,
just as you are in fact unleavened.
For [Messiah] our Passover also has been sacrificed.
Therefore let us celebrate the feast, not with old leaven,
nor with the leaven of malice and wickedness, but with
the unleavened bread of sincerity and truth.

—1 Corinthians 5:7–8

CONTENTS

Note to the Reader and Acknowledgments

This book is a labor of love! Like so many other significant achievements, if you asked us how long it took to produce this volume, Darrell and I would have to respond, "A lifetime!" I was raised in a more traditional Jewish home, and Darrell Bock, who also is Jewish by birth, has been plumbing the depths of the life of Jesus far more deeply than I ever could.

However, this book and its larger companion volume, *Messiah in the Passover,* did actually take almost two years to produce. Our contributing authors first composed their work and then we all met together in Los Angeles for three days of peer review where we critiqued one another's chapters, chuckled at one another's mistakes (especially those created by Microsoft Word's auto-correct feature), and prayed with and for one another. Our fervent hope is that the Lord would use this book to glorify the Lamb of God who takes away the sin of the world (John 1:29).

Our Thanks to You and Your Family

Most of all, we are grateful to the Lord and to our beloved Messiah Jesus, whom we also call Yeshua, which is His proper Hebrew name. We are also thankful for each disciple of the Messiah who reads this book because by doing so, you are expressing interest in the Jewish roots of your faith. We have written this particularly for you who know Him because He abides with you and will always be with you and in you (Matt. 28:20; John 14:17).

We are also so thankful for each skeptic or spiritual seeker who reads this book—whether you are Jewish or Gentile, and whether you read it out of curiosity or because someone dared you to, or for any other reason—because when all is said and done, our heart's desire and prayer to God for you is that you draw closer to God though the Messiah.

So whoever you are, dear reader, we want to acknowledge our gratitude to you, as you and your family are the very reason we took the time to produce this work.

Our Thanks to Chosen People Ministries

We are also grateful to Chosen People Ministries, the ministry that allows us to serve the Lord among the Jewish people. It also provides us with the inexpressibly precious opportunity to make "Messiah in the Passover" presentations at local churches and to lead Messianic Passover Seders at Messianic congregations. I presently serve as the president of Chosen People Ministries and Dr. Bock serves as a board member. Together we praise God for His faithfulness to this ministry and the opportunity to serve Him among the Jewish people.

Chosen People Ministries was founded in 1894, shortly after a Hungarian immigrant named Rabbi Leopold Cohn came to know the Lord in New York City. One of the objections Rabbi Cohn had before he received the Lord—and one that is so difficult for most Jewish believers in Jesus to overcome—is that he truly believed that if he accepted Jesus he would no longer be Jewish. Yet, nothing could be further from the truth. When I came to faith in Jesus the Messiah, I finally understood how faith in Him supplies the key to the Jewish identity I had always known and had sought to understand more fully. As the Bible came alive in a new way, the Exodus and the celebration of the Passover—it all became more meaningful when I recognized that these and other great events in our Scriptures pointed to the coming of the Messiah who died and rose to set us free from sin and death.

Passover, the subject of this book, is a powerful reminder that being Jewish and believing in Jesus go hand in hand. For this and many other reasons, we are grateful to our Messiah Yeshua for being the Passover Lamb who not only takes away the sin of the world, but who takes away our sins and puts them as far away from us *"as the east is from the west"* (Ps. 103:12).

OUR THANKS TO THE CONTRIBUTORS

There are many people who have contributed to this book and its larger companion volume, *Messiah in the Passover.*

I would of course like to thank the authors for their excellent contributions to the book. Their research, writing and dedication have been impressive all the way through the process.

I also want to thank those who contributed valuable editorial input—some of whom are on our board and staff, including Brian Crawford, Olivier Melnick and Robert Walter. A special thank you to board member Marion Wells for her diligent and thorough edits and for her participation in the peer review sessions in Los Angeles. I am also grateful for the help of Ala n Shore, one of our long-term staff members, who helped in some very critical areas.

My sincere thanks also to the Chosen People Ministries Publications Department led by Nicole Parramore, including graphic designers Maralynn Rochat Jacoby and Lois Gable Ruedinger.

The Scripture index was prepared by a team which included Elisabeta Pindic and Jeannie Goldstein, and proofreading was expertly done by Marcia Goldstein. We are so thankful for their efforts.

A special thank you goes to Paul Brinkerhoff of Grace and Truth Communications, our "super editor" who was so helpful and encouraging along the way. I think we have made him into an honorary Messianic Jew!

We also want to extend especially warm thanks to my assistant, Jacqui O'Rhea, who managed an exhaustive number of logistical necessities to prepare this and the companion book for publication.

Many thanks as well to Julia Freeman and the Chosen People Ministries Church Ministries staff who schedule thousands of presentations at local churches that enable us to teach so many people about the magnificent truths of Messiah in the Passover. Likewise, our thanks go out to the many pastors and ministry leaders who allow us to conduct "Messiah in the Passover" presentations for their congregations.

We must not forget the role of our mentors from previous generations, including Dr. Daniel Fuchs and Harold Sevener, who trained hundreds of Chosen People Ministries' staff to love the Passover and to teach these truths of redemption to others. Their work in the twentieth century helped shape our efforts in the twenty-first.

I also want to thank the Chosen People Ministries Board of Directors for their patience, understanding, and encouragement to make the truths of the Messiah in the Passover known through our ministry.

I know that Dr. Darrell Bock was supported as usual by his wife, Sally, who stands by his side in all of his many diverse projects . . . thanks, Sally, for keeping your brilliant husband on track!

Finally, I want to add a special thank you to the beautiful mother of my children, Dr. Zhava Glaser, who helped with the concept of these books, wrote a wonderful chapter for the companion volume, *Messiah in the Passover,* served as our resident Hebrew expert, and was deeply engaged in the book's production.

May the Lord bless you richly as you explore the truths of the Gospel in the Passover!

Mitch Glaser
New York City
April, 2017

CONTRIBUTORS

Larry Feldman has been working with Chosen People Ministries since 1974. He currently is the Southwest Area Director for both Chosen People Ministries and the Messianic Jewish Alliance of America (MJAA). He has also been serving as the president of the MJAA since 2015. He has planted or helped in establishing seven Messianic congregations from New York to California. Larry earned an Advanced Jewish Studies Degree from Moody Bible Institute as well as a Master of Theology from Dallas Theological Seminary with highest honors in Old Testament and Semitic Languages. Larry has been a Messianic Jew since 1972 and has been married to Fran for over forty years. He is currently leading the Messianic congregation he founded in 1997 called *Shuvah Yisrael* (Return O Israel), located in Irvine, California.

Mitch Forman was raised in a traditional Reform Jewish home near Boston. He attended the University of Massachusetts before pursuing a culinary career. Mitch went on to work in some of the finest hotels and restaurants in Boston and San Francisco, achieving his goal of cooking alongside the best chefs in the world. In 1987, Mitch came to faith in Jesus after talking with a Christian coworker about the Bible. He then became involved with Jewish outreach over the next twelve years, from San Francisco to New York City. In 2002, Mitch and his family returned to Boston, where he began teaching classes focused on the Jewish background of the Scriptures. He was also involved in the founding and leadership of Beth Yeshua Messianic Congregation in Newton, which is the heart of Boston's Jewish community. Mitch currently serves as the Vice President of U.S. Ministries for Chosen People Ministries, overseeing all recruitment, training, mentoring, and leadership of the entire U.S.-based missionary staff. Mitch is married to Kina, and they have two daughters and a son.

Richard E. Freeman was born and raised in Brooklyn, New York, in a very traditionally Jewish but nonreligious family. In 1973 Rich married his wife, Julia, who was from an Italian Catholic background. God reached Rich through Julia's spiritual pilgrimage, but not before Rich's Christian supervisor at work shared the Gospel with him. Rich received Yeshua as his Messiah in January of 1983. In September 1994, Rich earned a Master of Divinity degree from Conservative Baptist Seminary of the East, now part of Bethel Theological Seminary. He went on to earn a Doctor of Ministry degree from Gordon-Conwell Theological Seminary. Rich teaches on various topics such as Jewish evangelism, Messianic prophecy, end-time prophecy, the Church and Israel, the feasts of Israel, and more. He currently serves as the Vice President of Church Ministries and Conferences as well as the Southeast Regional Director for Chosen People Ministries. Rich and Julia have three children and five grandchildren and live in West Palm Beach, Florida.

Rachel Goldstein-Davis grew up in a Messianic home and watched her parents faithfully serve the Lord among the Jewish community. This instilled a passion for praying for and reaching out to her Jewish people and she felt called to commit her life to full-time outreach. Rachel received her undergraduate degree from Moody Bible Institute in 2002 in Jewish Studies and Bible. She joined the staff of Chosen People Ministries and served for five years in New York City. She loves to disciple children and youth, teaching young people to share their faith confidently with their Jewish friends. She also coordinates conferences for young Messianic believers around the globe as well as organizing short-term mission trips to Israel. In 2007, Rachel moved to Israel and received her citizenship, and is now serving at the Jerusalem and Tel Aviv Messianic Centers. Once in Israel, she met Steve Davis, a British Jewish believer who also felt the call from the Lord to live and serve in Israel. They have been married since June 2010 and have two young boys.

Cathy Wilson continues to draw Jewish and Gentile people to the Lord through performing comedic and dramatic sketches in the Phoenix metropolitan area. Although Cathy portrays Jewish characters, she grew up in a non-Jewish home in the Bronx, New York. While her home was "religious," she came to truly know the Lord during her senior year of high school. Cathy immediately applied to Northeastern Bible College in Essex Fells, New Jersey, and graduated in 1974 with a Bachelor of Arts in Biblical Literature. Cathy and her husband, Bob, lead a Jewish ministry team at Scottsdale Bible Church in Arizona. She trains the team to educate the Church about the Jewish roots of Christianity and to share the Gospel with Jewish people in the Phoenix area. Cathy has initiated a partnership between Scottsdale Bible Church and Chosen People Ministries to create Beth Sar Shalom, a monthly Messianic fellowship that invites Jews and Gentiles to worship the God of Abraham, Isaac, and Jacob together, through Jesus the Messiah.

INTRODUCTION:
THE GOSPEL IN THE PASSOVER

MITCH GLASER

The seven great festivals of the Jewish people, mostly found in Leviticus 23, usually point to something unique about the character of God and His purposes for humankind. They look back on the history of Israel, are often linked to the agricultural cycle, and more importantly point forward prophetically to the Messiah in the fulfillment of all of God's promises to the Jewish people.

The Jewish holidays include teaching, special sacrifices, eating unleavened bread, building booths, and the blowing of the shofar (ram's-horn trumpet). The seven great festivals of Israel are filled with object lessons that help us better understand the story of redemption. These object lessons, woven into the very fabric of the feasts, enable the Israelites to "get their hands a little dirty" and to not merely hear or listen, but to *do* and *participate* so that the lessons of the festivals became ingrained in their very souls. It's no secret to modern experts on the process of learning that it is not merely children who learn better by doing—but adults do as well. Participating in the activities makes these lessons unforgettable.

This is the foundation for the Passover: it is a festival filled with opportunities for participation in the remembrance of our great deliverance from Egypt. We were told to recount the story year after year so that new generations of Jewish people would never forget what God did in delivering the people of Israel from Egypt. There are symbols, given from Sinai that were part of the Torah, and instructions to the Jewish people on to how to observe the Feast. Jewish traditions have also grown up around these biblical injunctions to further help the Jewish people remember this most formative and critical event of the nation's history.

It is wonderful to observe the Passover because there are so many invaluable lessons preserved in the festival for the people of God. Jesus celebrated the Passover with His disciples in light of His sacrifice for our sins. Similarly, Christians throughout the world, in one way or another, remember Jesus and give thanks for His sacrificial death through the Lord's Supper, also called Communion or the Eucharist.

When Christians celebrate the Passover, however, they grow in their understanding of the Old Testament, affirm the Jewishness of the Gospel, deepen their understanding of the Lord's Supper, build community with fellow Christians, and develop a common experience that will enable them to better communicate the Gospel to their Jewish friends.

Most of all, when Christians celebrate the Passover, in one way or another, we are passing along the glorious message of redemption to future generations and linking our children and grandchildren to the Exodus. This will help our children develop a sense of continuity between the Old and New Testaments and between prophecy given and prophecy fulfilled. This will build the faith of our children, giving them greater assurance that what the Bible said about the future has and will come to pass.

The Last Supper and Jewish Tradition

One of the critical questions addressed in this book is, "How similar was the Last Supper celebrated by Jesus and His disciples to the modern-day Jewish Passover?"

Is today's Passover celebration a transparent window into the way in which Jesus and His disciples celebrated Passover? Did Jesus observe the same Jewish traditions as Messianic Jews who grew up in a Jewish home?

The clear answer to this question is, "We do not know." Additionally, we understand that this question is not only important for the Passover but for the entirety of the New Testament since it was penned within a Jewish historical context. In fact, whatever principles we determine regarding the role of Jewish tradition in first-century Jewish life—especially in the words and activities of Jesus and His disciples—will not only help guide us in understanding the Passover, but also many portions of the New Testament. There is no question that the New Testament is a very Jewish book and that in order to understand it properly, we must do our best to understand the culture and context of the time, which was both religiously and culturally Jewish.

While we cannot presume that today's Passover Haggadah can simply be read into the Last Supper, we do point out where we find striking parallels between the religious customs observed by Jesus at the Last Supper and later Jewish religious developments. Many of our authors (especially in the larger reference volume, *Messiah in the Passover*) will suggest that these traditions could have been practiced during the Last Supper.

We cannot assume that every author writing in this volume will be in agreement as to the degree that the later Jewish traditions can be read into the Last Supper. The editors of this book believe that it will be valuable for the reader to see these multifaceted opinions and then come to their own conclusions.

There is an old Jewish joke, which most Jewish people are well familiar with. It's usually told as an aphorism with a twinkle of the eyes and a smile: "Where there are two Jewish people, there are three opinions." We do not always like Jewish jokes, as sometimes they express prejudice towards Jewish people. But in this instance, the joke expresses a profound truth that is critical to understanding the book you are about to read. Jewish religious tradition prides itself on having a variety of viewpoints on the same issue, and Jewish people view this as healthy. This reflects our approach to the challenge of understanding the level at which later Passover traditions may be read into the final Passover of Yeshua the Messiah.

We do not want you to be confused, but it is important to understand that there are many different opinions within Jewish tradition, as you will see throughout the chapters of this book and its companion volume. Where possible, we have tried to align the various positions of the authors, but you should expect to find varying viewpoints. In summary, there is not just one answer to the question, "What traditions did Jesus and the disciples observe during the Last Supper"?

Our hope is that your reading of this book will be the beginning of a lifelong journey in exploring the ways in which Jewish religious tradition helps you better understand the life and times of Jesus the Messiah.

Passover as a Source of Types, Symbols, and Prophecies

The Exodus, the first (Egyptian) Passover, and subsequent Passovers are often used by the biblical authors to point towards a greater redemption. This is sometimes accomplished in the Scriptures through literary types, symbols, and prophecies. However, the Bible student must take great care in the ways biblical types and symbols are understood. There is no question that the Exodus and the first Passover look forward to similar but greater events, but care must be given in the interpretation of the various composite elements of the Exodus event. We should refrain from reading prophetic fulfillment into every aspect of the festival.

It is best, first of all, to understand the Exodus and first Passover as the participants might have viewed them at the time of the event. When interpreting prophecy, we should always consider the way in which the original hearers might have understood the prophetic word— even when the prophecy refers to future events the hearers might not expect nor understand. I am sure that the Israelites who were delivered from bondage did not realize that the lambs slain for the redemption of the firstborn nor the Exodus itself would have additional meaning in reference to an understanding of salvation or of the work of the future Messiah (1 Peter 1:10–12).

Yet, the Lord would fill these original events with greater meaning at a later day. But, this fulfillment could obviously only be understood in retrospect. For example, we would not suggest that the Israelites slaughtering the lamb for the first Passover in any way knew that the lamb would find ultimate fulfillment in the shed blood and sacrifice of Jesus. Yet, in hindsight we know this is true, which leads us to the second principle of interpretation we would suggest for you to consider.

A second rule of thumb is to view Passover and the Exodus as a type seen through the lens of the New Testament writers. Because the Apostles Peter, John, and Paul refer to various elements related to the observance of Passover as a foreshadow of the Messiah, we have a solid, biblical basis for looking back at these great events in the Old Testament and viewing them as types, symbols, and prophecies of events to come. Perhaps one of the clearest passages in the New Testament that helps us see this principle at work is in 1 Peter 1:18–19,

> *. . . knowing that you were not redeemed with perishable things like silver or gold from your futile way of life inherited from your forefathers, but with precious blood, as of a lamb unblemished and spotless, the blood of Christ.*

Our authors will help you discern how the Bible uses the Exodus and the Passover as types so that you will be careful not to go beyond the text, because we cannot simply interpret every detail as prophecy or we might find ourselves forcing Scripture to mean something that was never intended, just so it fits with a pattern we envision ourselves.

One might ask the question, "Did Moses have the sacrifice of Jesus in mind when he asked the children of Israel to offer a spotless, unblemished lamb and smear the blood of the lamb on the lintel and doorposts of their homes on the night when the firstborn of Egypt were judged?" This remains to be seen as we journey through this book, but for now, you might consider the following: it seems that the writers of the New Testament understood the Passover and the sacrifice of a lamb in this Messianic way—especially John the Baptist, who cried out, *"Behold, the Lamb of God who takes away the sin of the world"* (John 1:29). Yet, there is much more to be uncovered!

Some of our authors believe that the way the lamb was selected is also prophetic of the schedule Jesus kept during the last week of His life and that the choosing and testing of the lamb and the time of the lamb's sacrifice follow the dates of the Jewish calendar as well, making the calendar itself prophetic.

Many scholars also see the seven days of Unleavened Bread (a separate biblical feast that occurs immediately after Passover and is often combined and discussed with it) fulfilled in the perfect, sinless life Jesus lived before He was crucified. How purposeful was God in linking the Messiah to the Jewish calendar? Most believers in Jesus see these links, but how can we know that seeing the feasts fulfilled in Jesus to this degree is a correct biblical interpretation? These are some of the questions we will try to answer throughout this book, with even more attention given in the larger reference volume, *Messiah in the Passover* (more on this below).

Some of your ideas about the Passover will be reaffirmed in reading this present book and in other areas you will be challenged! Our prayer is that you will be open to the Lord and to the Scriptures and read the chapters with an open Bible, using great discernment so that you will learn more and that your faith will grow through better understanding the redemption we enjoy through Jesus the Messiah.

THE FESTIVALS AS A ROADMAP TO REDEMPTION

It is as impossible to study the Passover in a vacuum, as it is the first festival among the seven great holy days detailed by God in Leviticus 23. It would be difficult to understand

Passover without the associated festivals of Unleavened Bread, First Fruits, and the Feast of Weeks. These four festivals make up the first section of the festivals listed in Leviticus 23 and fall within the first few months of the Hebrew calendar. The final three festivals—the New Year, the Day of Atonement, and the Feast of Tabernacles—are observed in the seventh month of the Jewish calendar, which is a lunar calendar, not a solar calendar like our own.

The seven great festivals of the Jewish year—and the weekly Sabbath—look back at a great event in biblical history, are often tied to the agricultural calendar of Israel, and call for various ceremonies and sacrifices to bring attention to the theme of a given festival. They also seem to point to a greater fulfillment. Leviticus 23 itself does not inform us of this greater fulfillment, but other Scriptures in the Old and New Testaments do.

As you will see in reading through the various chapters, Passover is clearly used by the biblical authors to point to something greater. Commonly, the first four spring festivals point to the first coming of Jesus and the last three festivals in the seventh month are usually associated with His second coming. Once again, we understand this from later passages in the Old and New Testaments. You will not find this taught in the earlier chapters of the Torah—including Leviticus 23, as we understand this in retrospect through the words of Jesus and the actions of the writers of the New Testament. As you will read, Passover is the clearest and most common festival to be understood by the New Testament writers as being fulfilled in the person and work of Jesus. Yet, the other festivals are alluded to in various ways as well.

ENJOY THE FESTIVAL AND THE BOOK

Will we be celebrating Passover this year? Of course! As believers in Jesus the festivals are more meaningful to us than ever before—especially Passover. We hope you and your family will find a way to celebrate the Festival as well.

During the Feast of Unleavened Bread, we are powerfully reminded of Jesus' sinless nature, purity, and innocence as we eat *matzah* (unleavened bread) and avoid bread made with yeast for seven days. Then there is the Passover Seder itself, which will give us a new and exalted view of Jesus, the Lamb of God who takes away the sin of the world. When we find the hidden piece of matzah called the *afikoman*, we can hear echoes of our Savior's voice reverberating through time as He tells His disciples at the Last Supper, *"This is My body which is given for you; do this in remembrance of Me"* (Luke 22:19). As we drink the four cups of the fruit of the vine, we will be especially drawn to the third cup when He said to His disciples *"This cup which is poured out for you is the new covenant in My blood"* (Luke 22:20).

Passover is more important to me now as a believer in Jesus than it was for me growing up in a traditional Jewish home. Passover has its natural and glorious fulfillment in Jesus the Messiah—the Lamb of God who takes away the sin of the world.

This book should be viewed as a guidebook filled with biblical, traditional, and practical information about the Passover. We have included a Messianic Family Haggadah with readings for the Passover Seder, along with many delicious Passover recipes so you can celebrate your own Passover. Also included are Passover lessons for your children or Sunday school class. You may be interested to know that this book, *The Gospel in the Passover,* is taken from a larger reference volume mentioned above, titled *Messiah in the Passover*, which includes a full complement of chapters on the biblical and theological, historical and traditional, and other Gospel-focused perspectives on the Passover—as well as more recipes! Additionally, we have created a Messiah in the Passover website (www.messiahinthepassover.com) that will enhance your experience of the book and further equip and guide you and your family to celebrate this great festival of Passover. But in this shorter work we present the core teachings about the Passover that will help you learn how to celebrate a Messianic Seder yourself. We will also help you learn how to share the message of the Gospel through the Passover.

May the Lord bless you as you dig into the Jewish roots of your faith and learn more about the Gospel in the Passover!

1

PASSOVER IN YOUR HOME

CATHY WILSON

When I first joined the staff of Chosen People Ministries, I didn't see why I should have to give "Messiah in the Passover" presentations in various churches and Bible study settings as a part of my ministry. "Maybe they would make an exception for me," I thought. "After all, I'm a Gentile! I never celebrated Passover. Why would I begin to commemorate this feast or teach others the ways in which Jesus fulfills the Passover?" But, my questions faded quickly once I began to understand the importance of Passover and the ways in which Jesus is present in the celebration of this holiday.

I am a Gentile believer in Jesus, but I have been grafted into the blessings of the Abrahamic Covenant (Gen. 12:1–3; Eph. 2:11–22). God tells Abraham that all the families of the earth will be blessed through the Messiah who will come through Jewish lineage. I have been personally blessed through the Promised One of Israel, the Jewish Messiah Jesus. The Jewish festivals are an important part of the Old Testament, and though Gentile believers are not required by covenant to observe them, I have chosen to better understand these holidays by celebrating them with my family—especially the Passover. This has already brought incredible enrichment to my life, and I am hoping that you will engage with these great festivals and find the same spiritual blessings I have enjoyed.

As I began to journey through the Scriptures, I asked the Lord, "What is the importance of the Passover festival in relation to Your plan for the world?" After months of intensive Bible study, the Lord began to answer my question. I began to understand the weighty implications of Passover in God's plan of redemption! And my family has been celebrating the Passover as fulfilled in Jesus the Messiah every year since my journey began. May I give you a few steps to take to begin your pilgrimage with the Passover?

PRAYER

How does a Gentile go about understanding and even hosting a Passover Seder? These questions can only be answered through prayer. Ask God to give you direction and an increased burden to begin the adventure of taking hold of your Jewish roots in Jesus. The Apostle Paul, who was Jewish, uses the illustration of an olive tree to explain this magnificent truth to the Gentile Christians in Rome, who were unaware of how deeply rooted their faith was in the Old Testament and that they were now grafted into covenants and promises God gave to the children of Israel.

> *But if some of the branches were broken off, and you, being a wild olive, were grafted in among them and became partaker with them of the rich root of the olive tree, do not be arrogant toward the branches; but if you are arrogant, remember that it is not you who supports the root, but the root supports you.* (Rom. 11:17–18)

This does not mean that Gentile (non-Jewish) believers have replaced the Jewish people, which is a false notion

the Apostle warns us against by encouraging Gentile
Christians to have a humble attitude. But what a joy it
is to realize that in the Messiah, both Jewish and Gentile
followers of Jesus share a rich faith heritage, of which
Passover is a vital part.

LOOKING BACK BUT MOVING FORWARD

In the Hebrew Scriptures and especially through the great
festivals of Israel, God calls upon the children of Israel to
remember what He has done on their behalf. He instructs
them to rejoice in His power to deliver and to thank Him
for His provision. He teaches His chosen people through
the words of His prophets to anticipate a glorious future
as well as the coming of the Promised One, the Messiah.
Repeatedly, God tells His people to remember the day
when He took them out of Egypt, as looking back
provides strength to go forward as His chosen beacon of
redeeming light to the nations.

I began to research the Passover with a view towards
celebrating the Feast as a follower of Yeshua. Since the
Jewish people celebrate Passover, I decided to begin
my search with the experts! I began by reading several
different versions of the *Haggadah*—the Passover Seder
guidebook, containing prayers, songs, and the account of
the first Passover in Egypt read by Jewish families during
the observance of the Festival. I poured over traditional
Jewish Haggadahs; I also perused Messianic Haggadahs
that were developed by Jewish believers in Jesus, which
showed the fulfillment of the Passover in Jesus the Messiah
and emphasized the link between the Passover, the Last
Supper, and Communion.

The staff of Chosen People Ministries has put together a
"Messianic Family Passover Haggadah" (see chapter 5).

You are permitted to make copies of the Haggadah from this book for use with your family, home group, or church to celebrate a Jesus-centered Passover Seder or go to www.messiahinthepassover.com and download a printable copy for those attending your Seder. We trust you will find our Haggadah's blend of traditional elements with its biblical and Messianic aspects especially fitting for all believers and friends and family who are not yet believers in Yeshua our Messiah.

When planning your menu for Passover, please make note of chapter 6, which contains recipes and will show you how to prepare the foods for the Passover meal. Consider joining together those with whom you fellowship who might help you in the preparation of your Passover Seder.

INVITING FAMILY: INCLUDING JEWISH PEOPLE WHO ARE NOT YET JESUS FOLLOWERS

A key Hebrew word for "feast" is מועד, *mo'ed*, which in passages such as Leviticus 23 means "appointed feast" or "appointed time" (vv. 2, 4, 37, 44). It also designates an "appointed place" or "place of assembly" such as the tent of "meeting" (Exod. 33:7).[1] What a beautiful picture of God's heart! God is a personal God whose desire is to meet with us for communion and fellowship. Celebrating the Passover and the other great festivals of Israel draws us closer to the Lord. Far from being a series of cold unfamiliar rituals, the Passover leads us to delight in His presence and understand His plan and purposes for our lives. After all, life begins with redemption—that's the day we were set free by the blood of the Lamb, our Savior and Messiah Jesus. Our lives are built upon the foundation of redemption.

---

1   Jack P. Lewis, "יעד [see under מועד]," *Theological Wordbook of the Old Testament*, ed. R. Laird Harris, Gleason L. Archer, and Bruce K. Waltke (Chicago: Moody Press, 1980), 1: 388–389.

You can share this truth as you extend to Jewish and Gentile friends an invitation to gather with you at your Passover Seder. The event is more than a religious ceremony and is designed have a deep and personal meaning for all who participate.

An Overview of the Passover

Should the Lord lead you to present a Passover Seder at your church or in your Bible study or home group, it is wise to consider including an introduction about the significance of the Passover. You might even suggest that your fellowship invite a Chosen People Ministries staff person to instruct the group (www.chosenpeople.com/church). Our Church Ministries staff would be happy to speak with you, your group leader, or your pastor.

Allow me then to share some of what I tell those who are unfamiliar with Passover to interest them in learning more and even celebrating a Seder. You will help your believing friends by introducing them to this great opportunity to better appreciate redemption!

The Lamb: Center Stage

The Body of Christ, the Church, is in existence today because of Passover. Paul, the Apostle to the Gentiles, writes, *"Christ our Passover also has been sacrificed"* (1 Cor. 5:7). Passover, the first feast God gave to the children of Israel, focuses on redemption through the shed blood of the Passover Lamb. If you are a follower of Jesus, you know that the death and resurrection of Jesus is the very foundation of our faith.

At the first Passover in Egypt, lambs enter the lives of the family members and are scrutinized from the tenth until the fourteenth of the month of Nisan (Exod. 12:1–7). An attachment to the lamb, now part of the Jewish household, naturally develops. To help His people understand the cost and value of redemption, it may be that God's intention was for the lambs to be cherished and then later mourned.

Can you imagine what the children of Israel really thought about God's instructions? "We're to do—what? Why?" The children of Israel may not have remembered what God had so graphically conveyed about a lamb years ago when He called Abram to offer his *only* son as a burnt offering. The father and son climbed one of the mountains in the land of Moriah and Isaac asked about the whereabouts of the burnt offering. His father plainly stated, *"God will provide for Himself the lamb for the burnt offering, my son"* (Gen. 22:8).

But, what happened on that day? Where was the lamb that God promised? The Lord provided a ram caught in the thicket by his horns as a substitute for Isaac (v. 13). This may well have been the first substitutionary sacrifice in the Bible. If not, it nevertheless dramatically displayed the biblical theme of substitutionary sacrifice.

We see this pattern emerge again in the Exodus when the time came for the first Passover, as God requires another lamb to be slain and its blood smeared upon the lintel and doorposts of each Israelite home as a substitute for the death of the firstborn sons of Israel. If the Israelites obey, their firstborn sons will not need to die. For the Lord will go through the land of Egypt to smite all the firstborn sons of the Egyptians, but when He sees the blood on the lintel and on the two doorposts, the Lord will pass over the door and will not allow the destroyer to come into the Israelites' houses to smite them (Exod. 12:7, 12–13, 21–23).

The lamb of the Egyptian Passover presents a foreshadowing of the Lamb mentioned in the fifty-third chapter of Isaiah, where Isaiah speaks of a lamb to come as a substitute for His people, Israel:

> *But He was pierced through for our transgressions, He was*
> *crushed for our iniquities;*
> *the chastening for our well-being fell upon Him,*
> *and by His scourging we are healed.*
>
> *All of us like sheep have gone astray,*
> *each of us has turned to his own way;*
> *but the Lord has caused the iniquity*
> *of us all to fall on Him.*
>
> *He was oppressed and He was afflicted,*
> *yet He did not open His mouth;*
> *like a lamb that is led to slaughter,*
> *and like a sheep that is silent before its shearers,*
> *so He did not open His mouth.* (Isa. 53:5–7)

The theme of the sacrificial lamb continues through Scripture, but can only be fully appreciated by first understanding the original Passover. By retelling the Passover story during the Seder, we deepen our connection to both the people and God of Israel as we understand that the ultimate sacrificial lamb is Jesus Himself.

A MIXED MULTITUDE

Scripture tells us that there were other people who were delivered from Egypt along with the children of Israel. The Hebrews did not leave Egypt alone; there were some people from other nations who came along with them.

> *A mixed multitude also went up with them,*
> *along with flocks and herds, a very large*
> *number of livestock.* (Exod. 12:38)

"Mixed" simply means "not Israelite"! Egypt had conquered other lands and took captives as slaves. This mixed multitude was most likely comprised of people captured from other nations and enslaved by Egypt.

God chose the children of Israel to bless the world. God's plan is not limited to the descendants of Abraham, Isaac, and Jacob but includes *"all the families of the earth"* (Gen. 12:3). Both Israelites and some non-Israelites were redeemed that night through the blood of the Passover lamb! The first Passover was not limited to the Hebrews but also enjoyed by non-Hebrews as well. This is all the more true of the redemption purchased at Calvary by the shed blood of the Lamb of God. This message is so beautifully summarized in the well-known verse John 3:16—perhaps a New Testament version of Genesis 12:3.

> *For God so loved the world, that He gave His only begotten Son, that whoever believes in Him shall not perish, but have eternal life.*

THE CHURCH—GOD'S CURRENT REDEMPTIVE TOOL

Passover reveals God's heart for the world. The Lord's charge to the people of Israel to keep Passover as a memorial forever demonstrates His desire to make sure that His people continue to tell His story of redemption to future generations. God is currently using the Church comprised of Jewish and Gentile believers in Jesus, *"one new man"* (Eph. 2:15), to tell this same story. The Church is called to proclaim the message of redemption through Jesus, the Passover Lamb, to the entire world. We know from Scripture that the Lord does not want *"any to perish but for all to come to repentance"* (2 Peter 3:9).

The story of *the* Lamb, from Genesis 22 to Exodus 12 to Isaiah 53 and on through the inspired pens of the New Testament writers, contributes greatly to our understanding of God's plan of redemption outlined in Scripture.

God commands the children of Israel to observe Passover as an everlasting memorial (Exod. 12:14). *"You shall observe this event as an ordinance for you and your children forever"* (v. 24; cf. 17). The Hebrew word for "observe" is שמר, *shamar*, a root with the basic idea of "to exercise great care over."[2] Whereas elsewhere in the Bible this word literally means to keep, guard, or protect, here "it expresses the careful attention to be paid to the obligations of a covenant, to laws, statutes, etc."[3] Yet the literal sense informs the ceremonial sense. As God guards the homes marked by the blood of the lamb, so He calls His people to keep vigilant watch over the message of His redemption by remembering the Passover each year. The message of the Passover needs to be indelibly stamped on the minds and hearts of our future generations by an annual reenactment of the Exodus event through the Passover ceremony that engages the hearts, minds, and souls of participants.

Both Jewish and Gentile believers in Jesus can glean so much from celebrating this feast. It is a glorious way to remember the story of redemption and to share these eternal truths with others.

Passover is a beautiful home-based holiday and provides an ideal way to be spiritually enriched and to share your faith with your Jewish friends and others who do not know the Lord. We should especially encourage Jewish people we know to attend the Seder in our home. Try asking your Jewish friends if they will be celebrating the Passover meal. If they are planning to, talk with them about what you are learning about the Passover. If they are not

---

2 John E. Hartley, "שמר," *Theological Wordbook of the Old Testament*, ed. R. Laird Harris, Gleason L. Archer, and Bruce K. Waltke (Chicago: Moody Press, 1980), 2:939.

3 Hartley, *Theological Wordbook of the Old Testament*, 2:939.

planning to attend a Seder, then invite them to your home to celebrate! One rationale for inviting Jewish friends is to ask them to join your family Seder to help make sure you properly explain the Jewish traditions of the Passover. This will make them feel more comfortable in coming.

God desires that the world may know Him (John 17:23; cf. Isa. 43:9–10). In addition to using the Messianic Haggadah mentioned earlier (see chapter 5), you might speak to your guests some of the words in the narrative section that follows, starting with "The Telling." Partake together of the Passover Seder plate and explain what each element represents. Remember, your Jewish friends can help with this. Rejoice with each other *"that Christ has become a servant to the circumcision on behalf of the truth of God to confirm the promises given to the fathers, and for the Gentiles to glorify God for His mercy"* (Rom. 15:8–9).

The Apostle John, who was given a unique and extended revelation of Jesus much like the prophets Daniel and Ezekiel, writes,

> *Then he showed me a river of the water of life, clear as crystal, coming from the throne of God and of the Lamb . . . There will no longer be any curse; and the throne of God and of the Lamb will be in it, and His bond-servants will serve Him.* (Rev. 22:1, 3)

As redeemed Jews and Gentiles, we will rejoice before the risen Lamb forever! The Lamb is not only for a person, a family, a nation, and the world; the Lamb is for eternity. What a delight to meet with God and honor Him during the feast of Passover in our homes today in preparation for the great day coming!

The following narrative may help you explain the Passover Seder and the grand story of redemption beginning with the Exodus and first Passover and incorporating the Jewish traditions surrounding Passover viewed in light of Jesus the Lamb of God. I hope this will help you tell this wonderful story to your family and all who are willing to learn more about the Jewish Messiah.

You may simply adapt this narrative as a Bible study to be used with the traditional Seder symbols as object lessons, or you may use parts of this narrative as a backdrop to help you present a Seder, especially if you have not done this previously. If you provide participants with a copy of "A Messianic Family Haggadah" for reference during the Seder (see chapter 5), you do not need to read all of this, but you (and they) may find the information in the narrative helpful as you fill in the gaps of the story presented in the Haggadah.

We hope you will find creative ways to use this narrative with both young and old!

THE TELLING (*HAGGADAH*)

It's Passover! Welcome to God's Passover table. God told the Jewish people to keep Passover as a memorial—forever! He told them to remember His mighty deeds on their behalf—His deliverance from the bondage in Egypt. Passover is central to God's plan of redemption for the world!

UNLEAVENED BREAD

At Passover in Jewish homes, elaborate spring cleaning begins before the Feast. Foods containing *chametz* (leaven) are not allowed. The house must be cleaned and all leaven removed. Leaven is a symbol of sin in the Tanakh—the Hebrew Scriptures. When God commanded the children of Israel to leave Egypt, it was in haste. The dough was made without yeast, as they did not have time to prepare loaves for baking and rising before their escape.

The unleavened bread points to our Messiah, Jesus, and reminds us of His sinless purity and complete innocence as described by the prophet in Isaiah 53:5–6,

> *But He was pierced through for our transgressions,*
> *He was crushed for our iniquities;*
> *the chastening for our well-being fell upon Him,*
> *and by His scourging we are healed*
>
> *All of us like sheep have gone astray,*
> *each of us has turned to his own way;*
> *but the* LORD *has caused the iniquity of us all*
> *to fall on Him.*

At Passover, the Papa, according to Jewish tradition, personally inspects each room to make sure that all *chametz* is removed. He gathers the family together and they walk from room to room; and by the light of a wax candle they search for the leaven. Light exposes sin. Who is the Light of the world? Jesus! (See John 8:12) Traditionally the Papa is equipped with a large feather and a wooden spoon to collect any crumbs. Crumbs of leaven, a symbol of sin in the Hebrew Scriptures, are collected on a wooden spoon to make sure it does not touch the collector who would then be defiled by the leaven.

The Mama will sometimes leave a little leaven on the kitchen windowsill and will always act surprised when the Papa finds it. It makes him feel important and it makes the children laugh. It's good to begin the feast of Passover with merriment and joy!

With all the crumbs of leaven collected on the wooden spoon, the Papa will then take the leaven and the spoon, wrap them in a linen cloth, and join the other Jewish men in the community in burning the leaven. The fire speaks of purging and purity, as the home must be leaven-free for the Feast of Unleavened Bread.

LIGHTING THE CANDLES

Once the leaven has been removed, the Passover Feast can begin. Mama kindles the Passover candles on the Seder table and recites a blessing in Hebrew welcoming the festival to her home. Light is a symbol of God's presence (Exod. 3:2; 24:17). Lighting candles during Jewish holidays is a constant reminder that God is light.

The beautiful prayer in Hebrew, with a phonetic English transliteration for pronunciation, is as follows,

בָּרוּךְ אַתָּה אֲדֹנָי אֱלֹהֵינוּ מֶלֶךְ הָעוֹלָם

אֲשֶׁר קִדְּשָׁנוּ בְּמִצְוֹתָיו וְצִוָּנוּ לְהַדְלִיק נֵר שֶׁל יוֹם טוֹב

Baruch atah Ado-nai Elo-hei-nu Me-lech
ha-Olam, asher kid-sha-nu bemits-vo-tav
vetsi-va-nu lehad-lik ner shel yom tov.

Translated into English, the words above mean,

> Blessed art Thou, O Lord our God, King
> of the universe, who has sanctified us with
> Thy commandments and commanded
> us to kindle the festival lights.

Some have asked, "Why does the woman light the Passover candles?" The Jewish woman has a very significant role in the religious Jewish home. The request to light the candles honors her. As Messianic Jews, we see something more! As the woman begins the Seder and gives light to the Passover table, so it was from the seed of a woman that the Messiah came to perform His redemptive ministry and bring light to the world (Gen. 3:15; Isa. 7:14; John 8:12).

The lighting of the candles initiates the Seder.

The term *Seder* means "order" and refers to the ensuing order of service for the Passover ceremony. The minimum requirement for observing the Passover is noted in God's instructions to the children of Israel found in Exodus 12:8,

> *They shall eat the flesh that same night, roasted with fire, and they shall eat it with unleavened bread and bitter herbs.*

The rabbis added additional elements including green vegetables, a roasted egg, *charoset*, and the four cups of wine. (The Seder plate and its elements will be discussed further below.)

On this night we will also enjoy the best meal of the Jewish year. Passover, like most of the biblical holidays, features special meaningful foods. This reminds us that, from a Jewish perspective, theology is not only taught, it is also eaten!

During the Seder, the Papa reads from the Haggadah. The Hebrew term *Haggadah* means "the telling," and the Hebrew word *Pesach* means "Passover," which comes from the verb *pasach*, "to pass over." During Passover we will retell the story of the way God passed over the firstborn sons of the children of Israel with the tenth plague and then delivered His chosen people from Egyptian bondage.

The Papa continues to share with his family from the Haggadah. He reads,

> Passover is an account of miraculous transitions from slavery to freedom, from despair to hope, from darkness to light. God's efforts to redeem Israel began that first night of Passover in Egypt. He

instructed the children of Israel that on the tenth
day of the month of Nisan a lamb was to be taken.

We read from Exodus 12:3–5 that the children of Israel were commanded to take a lamb from the flock and set it apart. The rest of the instructions regarding the lamb are found in Exodus 12:1–13. We will simply summarize the instructions given to the Israelites by God.

The lamb was to be an unblemished and perfect male and it was to become part of the family. What happens when you take an animal into your home? It's no longer just an animal. It becomes a pet. Can you imagine how the people felt when they brought the lamb into their home? It was *their* lamb! The next four days were a time to scrutinize the lamb and make sure it was without blemish. And then, if the lamb was spotless, they were commanded to kill it on the fourteenth day of the same month, as God instructed. Not a bone was to be broken and its blood was to be applied to the two doorposts and to the lintel of the house in which the Passover would be observed.

Further details are given in the remainder of Exodus chapter 12. God instructed the children of Israel to take a bunch of hyssop, which is an herb, a shrub used for purification rites. They were to dip that hyssop in the blood that was in the basin. The basin was probably the threshold or ditch, which was dug in front of the doorways of the houses in Egypt to help prevent flooding. It appears that the children of Israel killed their Passover lambs by the door of their homes, outside the house. The blood from the slaughter ran into the depression and was smeared on each doorpost and lintel and then, with the blood already in the basin, the door was sealed on all sides.

What a prophetic portrait of redemption! On that first Passover night, the children of Israel blood-sealed their doors and found safety. The next morning they left Egypt and began their journey toward the land promised to them by God (Gen. 15:17–21).

Papa then reads from Exodus 12,

> *For I will go through the land of Egypt on that night, and will strike down all the firstborn in the land of Egypt, both man and beast; and against all the gods of Egypt I will execute judgments—I am the LORD. The blood shall be a sign for you on the houses where you live; and when I see the blood I will pass over you, and no plague will befall you to destroy you when I strike the land of Egypt.* (vv. 12–13)

> *For the LORD will pass through to smite the Egyptians; and when He sees the blood on the lintel and on the two doorposts, the LORD will pass over the door and will not allow the destroyer to come in to your houses to smite you.* (v. 23)

The Papa exclaims, "This was our deliverance! This was our redemption!"

THE FIRST CUP: THE CUP OF SANCTIFICATION

Jewish people drink four cups of wine during the Passover Seder to commemorate the four aspects of redemption found in Exodus 6:6–7:

> *Say, therefore, to the sons of Israel, "I am the LORD, and I will bring you out from under the burdens of the Egyptians, and I will deliver you from their bondage. I will also redeem you with an outstretched arm and with great judgments. Then I will take you for My people, and I will be your God; and you shall know that I am the LORD your God, who brought you out from under the burdens of the Egyptians."*

We do not know when this tradition of the four cups was added to the Passover dinner, although we do find two cups delineated in the New Testament account of the Last Supper.

Papa pours the first cup and lifts it. This is the Cup of Sanctification, also called the Cup of Blessing. Sanctification means holiness or being set apart for an intended purpose. The first cup sets apart this meal to accomplish God's plans and purposes. Papa recites the blessing,

בָּרוּךְ אַתָּה אֲדֹנָי אֱלֹהֵינוּ מֶלֶךְ הָעוֹלָם בּוֹרֵא פְּרִי הַגָּפֶן.

Baruch atah Ado-nai Elo-hei-nu Melech
ha-Olam, bo-ray pri ha-gah-fen.

The English translation is,

Blessed art Thou, O Lord, our God, King of
the universe, Creator of the fruit of the vine.

On a night nearly two thousand years ago, a Passover Seder was conducted by a Rabbi among His followers in an upper room in Jerusalem. His name was Yeshua in Hebrew. Yeshua celebrated Passover at that Last Supper with His disciples. He lifted the first cup at the Passover that evening and recited the blessing in Hebrew. He then said, *"Take this and share it among yourselves."* And, Jesus and His disciples drank (see Luke 22:14–18).

THE WASHINGS

In Jesus' day and at the Passover Seder in Jewish homes today there are a number of washings. At the first hand washing, only Papa washes his hands. This sets him apart from the rest of the family. It shows that he has a significant role as the spiritual leader of the family. It was an ancient custom in that part of the world to wash one's hands before eating.

It was customary for a servant to perform this task of washing the hands. But Yeshua did something completely different by washing the feet of His disciples. This was an act of servanthood, performed to teach servanthood by example to His disciples. Yeshua even washed the feet of Judas Iscariot, the disciple whom He knew would betray Him later that evening!

THE SEDER PLATE

Papa turns his attention to the Passover plate upon which the various elements are situated: parsley, horseradish, lettuce, roasted egg, *charoset* (finely chopped apple mixture), and the shankbone of a lamb.

Papa lifts a sprig or two of parsley and reads from the Haggadah,

> This parsley which is green represents life, a renewed life. Life in Egypt during the time of the first Passover was a life of pain, suffering, and tears. The tears are represented by this salt water.

Yes, there was the hardship and the suffering in Egypt. Scripture tells us that Pharaoh made it difficult for the Jewish people. But there was also the renewal of life when God delivered the children of Israel from Egypt. Passover is observed in the spring when the earth is green with life after the deadness of winter. We see a resurrection in this celebration of Passover. Jesus rose from the dead on a day during the week of Passover! Passover is all about a renewed life and resurrection!

The family dips the parsley into a bowl of salt water and eats.

The Second Cup: The Cup of Plagues

Papa pours the second cup of wine, the cup of plagues or judgment. Everyone at the table dips their little finger into the wine ten times, reciting each of the ten plagues and dropping the wine on their plate: Blood! Frogs! Gnats! Flies! Pestilence! Boils! Hail! Locusts! Darkness! Death of the Firstborn!

This is very meaningful for a variety of reasons. Our action brings to life the holiness and judgment of God. It also reminds us that the wine that previously symbolized joy is reduced by a drop for every plague and thereby speaks of God's compassion for the Egyptians and our mercy as well toward those who suffer—even when they suffer as a result of what they have done to us.

The actual taking of the cup comes a bit later in the Passover Seder, and as far as we know this cup is not specifically mentioned in the New Testament accounts.

At this time in the Seder, the family sings a joyful song entitled *"Dayenu,"* which means "it is enough," or "we would have been satisfied." At the Passover Seder in Jewish homes, many verses of *"Dayenu"* are sung:

> If He had merely rescued us from Egypt,
>   but had not punished the Egyptians—*Dayenu*!

> If He had merely punished the Egyptians,
>   but had not destroyed their gods—*Dayenu*!

> If He had merely destroyed their gods,
>   but had not slain their firstborn—*Dayenu*!

> If He had merely fed us with manna,
>   but had not given us the Sabbath—*Dayenu*!

> If He had merely given us the Sabbath,
>   but had not brought us to Mount Sinai—*Dayenu*!

If He had merely brought us to Mount Sinai,
but had not given us the Torah—*Dayenu!*

If He had merely given us the Torah,
but had not brought us to the land of Israel—*Dayenu!*

If He had merely brought us to the land of Israel,
but had not built us the Temple—*Dayenu!*

We would have been satisfied!

Those of us who are Messianic believers, and recognize that Jesus is the Messiah, can add a further *Dayenu*, knowing that if God had only provided salvation through the death and resurrection of our Messiah, it would have been enough! But we know that He did much more. As Jesus says, *"I came that they may have life, and have it abundantly"* (John 10:10). He satisfies us and gives us a joy in living which can only come from trusting in Him.

On the tenth day of Nisan when all the lambs to be sacrificed were led into Jerusalem, Jesus, the perfect Passover Lamb, rode into Jerusalem on a colt of a donkey. For four days He lived with the community, and they scrutinized Him and found Him blameless, without blemish. Likewise, Pontius Pilate, Herod, the Sanhedrin, and the thief on the cross found no fault in Jesus.

And so, because Jesus was found to be perfect, on the fourteenth day of the month of Nisan, in accordance with Exodus 12, on the day of Passover, at nine o'clock in the morning, when the Passover lambs were tied to the altar in the Temple, Jesus, the sinless Son of God, was nailed to the cross. At three o'clock, when the priest slaughtered the last Passover lamb in the Temple, Jesus, our perfect Passover Lamb, the ultimate sacrifice for sin, cried from the cross, *"It is finished!"* and gave up His life for us. The debt was paid. Jesus fully satisfied God's righteous demands.

Was that the end? *No!* Three days later Jesus rose from the dead and conquered sin and death. And, it is because of Him that we can understand Passover, and it is enough! *Dayenu!*

THE MATZAH TASH

Papa then lifts the matzah tash, or the "Unity" as it is often called. The Unity holds three pieces of matzah. It seems strange that it should be called Unity and yet have three sections. Papa removes the matzah in the middle, raises it, breaks it in half, and says,

> This is the bread of affliction our fathers ate in Egypt. Let all who are hungry come and eat. Let all who are in need come and celebrate Passover.

Today in Jewish homes, the Papa takes one half of the middle piece of matzah, wraps it in a linen napkin, and hides it. After dinner the children search for it, find it, and raise it from its hiding place. This buried and raised middle piece of matzah is called the *afikoman*.

Jewish tradition tells us that the three pieces of matzah represent Abraham, Isaac, and Jacob, or perhaps the three classes of Jewish people: the priests, the Levites, and the common people of Israel. However, some Messianic Jews also suggest that the three pieces of matzah placed in one pouch remind us of the unity of God who reveals Himself in three persons: Father, Son, and Holy Spirit.

Admittedly, this reads meaning into the ceremony, as Judaism does not teach that God is triune in nature, and so we hold this interpretation with great humility. However, it is true that there is tremendous discussion among the rabbis as to why there are three pieces of matzah, what the names of these pieces are, what they represent, and why the middle piece of matzah is broken,

47

wrapped, hidden, and brought back at the end of the Passover Seder.

In following through with the idea that the three pieces of matzah reflect the triune nature of God, and the middle piece represents the Son of God, then the meaning of the breaking of the middle piece of matzah is even more significant. Once again, this is not taught within Judaism but is an interpretation that has developed among Messianic Jews over the years.

There is more to come regarding the afikoman at the conclusion of the Seder.[4]

The Four Questions

The youngest child asks the *four questions* that need to be asked at the Passover table. Prior to the first question, an opening question is asked, which in Hebrew is,

מַה נִּשְׁתַּנָה הַלַּיְלָה הַזֶּה מִכָּל הַלֵּילוֹת?

Mah nish-ta-nah ha-lai-lah ha-zeh mi-kohl ha-lay-lot?

In English, "Why is this night so different from all other nights?" Papa then answers from the Haggadah, "On this night we celebrate the going forth of the children of Israel from slavery into freedom."

Child: "On all other nights we eat bread with leaven. On this night why do we eat only matzah?"

Papa: "When Pharaoh let our forefathers go from Egypt they were forced to flee in great haste. As the children of Israel fled from Egypt they did not have time for their dough to rise. The sun, which

---

4   For more on the afikoman tradition, including its origin and role in the Passover, see *Messiah in the Passover* companion book, chapter 11, "Passover and the Afikoman," by Daniel Nessim.

beat down on the dough as they carried it along, baked it into unleavened bread called matzah."

Child: "On all other nights we eat all kinds of vegetables; on this night why do we eat only bitter herbs?"

Papa: "On Passover we eat only bitter herbs because our forefathers were slaves in Egypt and their lives were made very bitter."

Child: "On all other nights we never think of dipping herbs in water or in anything else; why on this night do we dip the parsley in salt water?"

Papa: "We dip the parsley in salt water because it reminds us of a renewed life that we longed for following a life of pain, suffering, and tears."

Child: "On all other nights we eat either sitting or reclining; on this night why do we eat only reclining?"

Papa: "Reclining was a sign of a free man long ago, and since our forefathers were freed on this night, we recline at the table."

In response to the four questions, the leader of the Seder will continue to tell the story of redemption—with both brief answers and lengthy readings from the Bible and Jewish tradition—all part of the service detailed in the Haggadah.

The Horseradish: Maror

Papa, lifting the horseradish, the *maror*, reads the following,

As sweet as our lives are today, let us remember how bitter life was for the children of Israel in the land of Egypt. As we dip the matzah into the bitter herbs, the maror, let us allow the bitter

taste to cause us to shed tears of compassion
for the sorrow that our ancestors knew.

Papa then reads,

> The children of Israel made bricks for Pharaoh's
> cities. We remember this task with a mixture of
> apples, cinnamon, nuts, and wine called *charoset*.
> Let us dip the matzah into the charoset and
> remember the hardships the Israelites endured
> under the whips of Pharaoh's taskmasters. But
> its sweetness will remind us of the freedom
> that was ours through God's deliverance.

The family dips their matzah into the apple mixture. As
followers of the Jewish Messiah Jesus, we are reminded
that even in the midst of bitter times, our lives are kept
sweet through our relationship with the Lord.

The Beitzah: Roasted Egg

Papa turns his attention to the roasted egg on the Seder
plate and reads,

> On the Seder plate there is a *beitzah*, a
> roasted egg. The egg speaks of a Festival
> (*hagigah*) sacrifice which can no longer be
> made because the Temple was destroyed.

Strange, you might think, that an egg is used to represent
this sacrifice. An egg usually represents life, but there is
more to it. According to tradition, the egg reminds us
of the daily sacrifices offered in the Temple. It is roasted
brown because the sacrifices were roasted. The rabbis
added the egg to the Seder plate after the destruction of
the Temple in 70 A.D. The egg is an annual reminder of
that future day when the Messiah will establish His throne
in Jerusalem, rebuild the Temple, and reintroduce the

Temple sacrifices. We believe that this great day is coming, but we also understand that the once-for-all sacrifice for sin through Jesus the Messiah has already been made, and the future Temple will honor His sacrifice.

THE SHANKBONE OF A LAMB: THE ZEROAH

Papa next turns his attention to the shankbone of the lamb on the Seder plate and reads,

> On the Seder plate there is a shankbone of a lamb. This roasted shankbone represents the lambs whose blood marked the houses of the children of Israel. Since the Temple in Jerusalem no longer stands, lamb is not eaten at Passover by Ashkenazic Jews, though lamb is eaten by Sephardic Jews—from Spain, North Africa, etc. This shankbone reminds us of the sacrificial lambs.

The Hebrew name for the shankbone is *zeroah*, which literally means "arm." The zeroah speaks of the outstretched arm of the Lord by which He redeemed His people from Egypt (Deut. 26:8). Messianic Jews link the term *zeroah* with the lamb who comes to save us from sin and death as the word is used in the Servant Song of Isaiah beginning in Isaiah 52:7 and concluding in chapter Isaiah 53:12. We believe this great passage speaks of the coming Messiah, so we view the saving arm of God as fulfilled in the Lamb of God—Jesus.

> *The LORD has bared His holy **arm***
> *in the sight of all the nations,*
> *that all the ends of the earth may see*
> *the salvation of our God.* (Isa. 52:10, emphasis added)

> *Who has believed our message?*
> *And to whom has the **arm** of the LORD been*
> *revealed?* (Isa. 53:1, emphasis added)

There is no Temple in Jerusalem today, no altar, and no sacrifice for sin as God commanded. How then can sins be forgiven? We find in Leviticus 17:11 that God tells the children of Israel,

> *For the life of the flesh is in the blood, and I have given it to you on the altar to make atonement for your souls; for it is the blood by reason of the life that makes atonement.*

God still requires the shedding of blood for the forgiveness of sin. It is the blood that makes atonement for the soul. Atonement means a covering for sin. This is God's provision.

The blood of the Passover lamb on the doorposts physically saved Israel that first Passover night and allowed them to begin their journey to the Promised Land. The blood of the perfect Passover Lamb, Jesus, saves us internally. He changes our hearts. When we trust in Messiah Yeshua we receive God's gift of salvation, which includes forgiveness of sins as well as eternal life.

Again, remember that the first Passover in Egypt not only included the children of Israel but Gentiles as well (Exod. 12:38). What a glorious picture of God's plan of redemption for the world!

THE THIRD CUP: THE CUP OF REDEMPTION

After the third cup is poured, Papa reads,

> God promised that He would return His people from slavery, that He would redeem His people with an outstretched arm.

It is this cup after supper in the Upper Room that Jesus raised and drank, which the Gospel writer describes in Luke 22:20:

> *And in the same way He [Yeshua] took the cup after*
> *they had eaten, saying, "This cup which is poured*
> *out for you is the new covenant in My blood."*

Our Messiah came. He died, shedding His blood to make atonement for sins. He is the perfect Passover Lamb. Through His outstretched arms on the cross, He provides redemption from sin and death forever, for any and all— Jew or Gentile—who place their faith and trust in Him.

We are not sure how much of the Passover tradition was developed at the time of Jesus, but we do know that He used this cup (which according to ancient tradition would have been the third cup) to join together the backdrop of the Passover with the promise of the New Covenant spoken of by the prophet Jeremiah in Jeremiah 31:31–34.

THE HIDDEN MATZAH: AFIKOMAN

After dinner, the children look for the *afikoman*. The wrapped matzah is raised from its hiding place and a prize is given to the child who finds it.

Prior to the Temple's destruction in 70 A.D., Jewish people ate the Passover lamb during the Passover Seder. No other solid food was to be eaten after eating the Passover lamb. Today Jewish people partake of the afikoman as the last solid food of the Seder.

After taking the cup with His disciples, Jesus institutes a further memorial using the afikoman to represent His own body. In Luke 22:19, the Gospel writer says,

> *When He had taken some bread and given*
> *thanks, He broke it and gave it to them, saying,*
> **"This is My body which is given for you;**
> **do this in remembrance of Me."**

Matzah is both striped and pierced. According to Isaiah 53, the Messiah will be both striped and pierced (v. 5). The Gospels tell us that Jesus' body was scourged for us; His body was pierced for us. Additionally, matzah is a food without leaven. Remember, leaven is a symbol for sin in the Scriptures. The matzah speaks of the sinless, perfect life of the Messiah who came to fulfill all righteousness. At His death, Jesus' body was wrapped in a linen cloth as is the afikoman. Jesus' body was buried in a tomb, just as the afikoman is hidden by the Papa during the Seder. Jesus' body was raised as the afikoman is found and raised from its hiding place by the children after dinner. Papa then breaks the afikoman in small pieces and distributes the pieces for each person to eat.

THE FOURTH CUP: THE CUP OF PRAISE

The fourth cup is called the Cup of Praise, or the Cup of Rejoicing, and the same prayer that has been sung over the first three cups is once again chanted by the Papa. We believe Jesus and His disciples also took the fourth cup as they left the Upper Room, singing a song from Psalm 118! Verse 24 of this psalm says, *"This is the day which the LORD has made, let us rejoice and be glad in it."* This may have been what Jesus sang as He made His way with the disciples to the Garden of Gethsemane and ultimately to the cross.

Papa reads as he takes the fourth cup,

> With this cup God is saying, "I will take you to Me for a people." This speaks of the time when the Lord will gather Israel.

The family then drinks the fourth cup.

The Fifth Cup: The Cup of Elijah

In Jewish homes today, the Papa continues to read from the Haggadah and notes the fifth cup of wine,

> We have a place setting that has not been touched. This is the place setting for Elijah. This cup is for Elijah. Where is Elijah? He is not here.

Each year in Jewish homes during the Passover, the door is opened to look for Elijah and invite him to join the Seder. When he is not there, Papa reads,

> Each year we pray that Elijah would come to the Seder, bringing a time of peace and freedom, bringing the time of the Messiah.

This coming of Elijah was predicted by the Prophet Malachi (see chapters 3 and 4 of the book of Malachi) and reaffirmed by Jesus when He told His disciples that John the Baptist came performing the ministry of Elijah, turning *"the hearts of the fathers to their children and the hearts of the children to their fathers"* (Mal. 4:5–6).

There is actually a charming tradition whereby Papa sends the children to the front door of the house, which is opened wide, and the children invite the prophet to sit down at the table and drink the wine and share the sumptuous feast. The participants at the Seder also sing a mournful and soulful song entitled "Elijah the Prophet," asking the prophet to come and bring the One Israel has been waiting for—the Messiah, the Son of David.

So far, however, there has only been disappointment, and the Cup of Elijah has been poured out into the sink. Yet, there is always hope expressed in the concluding song of the Seder,

לְשָׁנָה הַבָּאָה בִּרוּשָׁלַיִם!

L'shanah HaBa'ah B'Yerushalayim!

"Next Year in Jerusalem!"

The Conclusion of the Seder

The Passover Seder is now complete, even as our salvation and redemption are complete because the Messiah Jesus has fulfilled the Passover. He is our Passover who has been sacrificed for us (1 Cor. 5:7)!

Jewish people are still waiting for their Messiah. How important it is for us to tell our Jewish friends and neighbors that the Messiah has already come and that through Yeshua we can experience the fullness of personal redemption.

Celebrating Passover is a wonderful way to demonstrate the unity of Scripture and to give us a deeper understanding of the history of redemption culminating in the death and resurrection of our Messiah Jesus. We look back to look forward, and because of what God has done we are assured that He will accomplish what He promised. This includes the return of the Messiah Jesus and even the restoration of His chosen people by turning their hearts to His Son. Paul attests to this in Romans 11:25–27, that one day God's chosen people will recognize that Jesus is *the Lamb of God who takes away the sin of the world!*" (John 1:29).

Now you are better equipped to tell this glorious story and to share the Good News of Passover with both Jews and Gentiles!

2

JESUS, THE LAMB OF GOD

RICHARD E. FREEMAN

Have you ever noticed how often lambs or sheep are mentioned in the Bible? The title "Lamb of God" has become an important part of our common understanding of the person and work of Jesus the Messiah. John the Baptist sees Jesus approaching the Jordan River and cries out, *"Behold, the Lamb of God who takes away the sin of the world!"* (John 1:29).

The fifty-third chapter of Isaiah, a passage sometimes called the Gospel in the Old Testament, describes Jesus the Servant of the Lord in this way, *"Like a lamb that is led to slaughter, and like a sheep that is silent before its shearers, so He did not open His mouth"* (Isa. 53:7). This is the passage the Ethiopian eunuch is reading when Philip preaches Jesus to him (Acts 8:32–35). The book of Revelation uses the term "Lamb" to describe Jesus more than thirty times. Jesus and the term "Lamb" are intrinsically related, and the connection point is Passover. There is also an amazing prophetic parallel between the last week of Jesus and the story of the first Passover as found in Exodus 12.

A Lamb for Each Household

The story of the Passover begins with careful instructions given to the Israelites regarding a lamb. Moses writes,

> *Speak to all the congregation of Israel, saying, "On the*
> *tenth of this month they are each one to take a lamb*
> *for themselves, according to their fathers' households,*
> *a lamb for each household."* (Exod. 12:3)

The children of Israel are told here to choose a lamb and bring it into the household on the tenth day of the first month, which is the Hebrew month of Nisan. There is a difference of opinion among commentators as to whether there was a day on which a lamb was selected prior to it being brought into the household. Some say a lamb was selected on the ninth of Nisan and then brought into the household on the tenth day; others say a lamb was selected on the same day it was brought into the household, both occurring on the tenth of Nisan. A lamb was selected and brought into the house on the tenth day of Nisan.

The next set of instructions involved the community. Moses continues,

> *Now if the household is too small for a lamb, then he and*
> *his neighbor nearest to his house are to take one according*
> *to the number of persons in them; according to what each*
> *man should eat, you are to divide the lamb.* (Exod. 12:4)

Family units are commanded here to come together and feast upon the lamb. But if a family unit does not exist and there are perhaps only two single people, who probably cannot eat an entire lamb, then the family units are allowed to include others and this newly combined community will share it. The lamb belongs to this newly combined community. Moses adds a qualification regarding the health and age of the lamb,

Your lamb shall be an unblemished male a year old;
you may take it from the sheep or from the goats.
You shall keep it until the fourteenth day of the same
month, then the whole assembly of the congregation
of Israel is to kill it at twilight. (Exod. 12:5–6)

This is all very personal as indicated by the change in pronoun. The instructions begin with selecting "a lamb." Then with the combining of smaller households to make one community, "a lamb" becomes identifiably, "the lamb." Finally, "the lamb" becomes "your lamb," marking the animal as part of the particular community. The Passover is intended to be very personal and yet also an event and experience shared by the entire community.

THE FIRST PASSOVER

Imagine what this first Passover might have looked like more than three thousand years ago. The Exodus from Egypt is finally at hand after four hundred years of slavery. Nine horrific plagues have all but devastated the land of Egypt, and the people of Israel hold their breath with great anticipation, wondering what Moses will do next. Word comes to the people that a tenth plague will be the last and they should be prepared to leave.

Imagine now that it is the tenth day of Nisan and the family is gathered together in their dwelling: Mom, the children, and Dad. Then Papa, the head of that family and of the little community, brings the little lamb that was selected into the house. The children are excited about their new pet! Papa on the other hand is somber. He knows what is in store for this newest member of the family and community. For Moses has told the people,

"You shall keep [the lamb] until the fourteenth day of the same month, then the whole assembly of the congregation of Israel is to kill it at twilight." (Exod. 12:6)

The lamb is to be unblemished, with no imperfections whatsoever. In order to determine that this lamb is unblemished and without imperfections, the fathers, the heads of those little communities, have to watch their lambs interact within the community. They have to be sure that the lamb is perfect in order for it to be the sacrifice that will save them from the last plague. Imagine how hard it must have been for the children (and adults) to care for this animal, treat it like a pet, and then watch it die and eat it. But that is exactly what will happen, and ultimately the fathers and the leaders of various households will have to acknowledge that the lambs are worthy to be slain. The whole assembly of the congregation of Israel will kill the lambs all at the same time, at twilight, as though all the lambs are killed as one.

The time for redemption is at hand. The destroyer, the one who will kill each and every firstborn in Egypt, is on his way. The only way for the firstborn males to be saved from this last deadly plague is through obeying God and smearing the blood on the door so that the destroyer will see the blood of the lamb and pass over the home, saving the inhabitants from this plague. Passover paints a prophetic picture pointing to the day Jesus the Messiah will die as the Passover Lamb, the One who takes away the sin of the world.

The instructions God gives Moses for the Israelites regarding the placement of the blood requires a certain plant:

You shall take a bunch of hyssop and dip it in the blood which is in the basin, and apply some of the blood that is in the basin to the lintel and the two doorposts; and none of you shall go outside the door of his house until morning (Exod. 12:22).

The hyssop plant functions like a natural paintbrush. It has a long stem with a brushlike ending. It was used to sprinkle the blood in ordinary purifications (Lev. 14:51; Num. 19:18). In Psalm 51, David's psalm of repentance, David writes, *"Purify me with hyssop, and I shall be clean"* (v. 7). Here in Exodus 12:22 the instructions are to *"dip it in the blood [of the lamb] which is in the basin."* There are two thoughts as to what the basin is.

One, according to Targum Jonathan, is that the basin is an earthen vessel, into which the blood of the lamb is received when slain, and therefore is placed at the bottom of the door, and the precious blood of the lamb is not trampled upon (Targum Pseudo-Jonathan 12:22).

Two, the Hebrew word for "basin," בסף, *bassaph*, can also be translated "threshold." Therefore, the blood of the slain lamb runs into the threshold by the bottom of the door and pools in this natural basin. Either way the picture is similar. The hyssop plant is dipped in a pool of blood at the bottom of the doorframe. The brush of hyssop, now covered with blood, is applied by the Israelite to the lintel and doorposts per Moses' instructions to *"apply some of the blood that is in the basin to the lintel and the two doorposts"* (Exod. 12:22).

Some interpreters through the years have envisioned this act as tracing a bloody cross on the door of the home. Whereas we cannot demonstrate this from the text in Exodus, we do believe that in light of (1) Leviticus 17:11, which notes that *"the life of the flesh is in the blood,"* and (2) the foreshadowed death of Jesus as the Lamb of God who takes away the sin of the world, the image created by the blood on the door of the home points in a beautiful way to the future redemption available to all by faith in the shed blood of the Messiah Jesus. When by faith we accept Him as our Savior, then the blood of the Lamb covers our hearts as the blood of that little lamb in Exodus covered the homes of the Israelites acting in faith and obedience to what God commanded.

JESUS CAME TO BETHANY

John 12 parallels Exodus 12 and begins with this temporal note, establishing a time frame for the events that follow:

> *Jesus, therefore, six days before the Passover, came to Bethany where Lazarus was, whom Jesus had raised from the dead.* (John 12:1)

Jesus enters Bethany and the home of Lazarus, Martha, and Mary, his friends. It is late in the day on Friday, the eighth of Nisan, six days before Passover, but before sunset when the Sabbath begins.

Lazarus is an anomaly to the crowds gathered in Bethany. He is the one Jesus raised from the dead after four days. According to a midrash or ancient rabbinical commentary written long before the first century, it was a Jewish belief that the soul stays near the body for three days after a person's death: "For three days the soul hovers over the grave, contemplating a return to the body, but once it sees that the facial color has faded, it goes away, never to return" (Genesis Rabbah 50:10). So probably the Jewish community in Bethany viewed Lazarus as having been dead long enough for his spirit to have returned to God. And now Jesus is coming over to his house to have a Sabbath dinner with him and his family!

As usual, Martha is serving and Mary is sitting at the feet of Jesus. The Jewish religious leaders in opposition to Jesus come to see both Jesus and Lazarus, who simply by being alive is a walking testimony of Jesus' Messianic authority. The dinner ends and the Jewish religious leaders decide to treat both Jesus and Lazarus as threats and begin plotting against them.

The action slows on the next day, which is the Sabbath (Saturday), the ninth day of Nisan. It picks up again on the tenth of Nisan, sunset Saturday to sunset Sunday. This is the day the Passover lambs are selected and brought into the households. We believe this is the very day Jesus enters Jerusalem, presenting Himself as Messiah and King and ultimately as the Lamb of God. John describes the scene in and around the bustling city that day:

> *On the next day the large crowd who had come to the feast, when they heard that Jesus was coming to Jerusalem, took the branches of the palm trees and went out to meet Him, and began to shout, "Hosanna! Blessed is He who comes in the name of the Lord, even the King of Israel." Jesus, finding a young donkey, sat on it; as it is written, "Fear not, daughter of Zion; behold, your King is coming, seated on a donkey's colt."* (John 12:12–15)

Why the palm branches? The palm branches are actually part of the celebration of the Feast of Tabernacles, which takes place in the seventh month.

This celebration is described for us in the Torah:

> *On exactly the fifteenth day of the seventh month, when you have gathered in the crops of the land, you shall celebrate the feast of the LORD for seven days, with a rest on the first day and a rest on the eighth day. Now on the first day you shall take for yourselves the foliage of beautiful trees, palm branches and boughs of leafy trees and willows of the brook, and you shall rejoice before the LORD your God for seven days.* (Lev. 23:39–40)

Why did the Jewish people link the Feast of Tabernacles and the coming of the Messianic King? Writing about the end of days when the King of Kings will be reigning on earth, the Prophet Zechariah says,

> And the LORD will be king over all the earth; in that day the LORD will be the only one, and His name the only one.
>
> ... Then it will come about that any who are left of all the nations that went against Jerusalem will go up from year to year to worship the King, the LORD of hosts, and to celebrate the Feast of Booths. (Zech. 14:9, 16)

Jewish tradition in the first century had already joined the Feast of Booths or Tabernacles with the coming of the Messiah and His ascending the throne of David in Jerusalem. As Jesus rides on the colt of the donkey, the people recognize the picture from Zechariah's prophecy,

> Rejoice greatly, O daughter of Zion!
>   Shout in triumph, O daughter of Jerusalem!
>
> Behold, your king is coming to you;
>   He is just and endowed with salvation,
>
> Humble, and mounted on a donkey,
>   Even on a colt, the foal of a donkey. (Zech. 9:9)

The crowds are shouting, *"Hosanna to the Son of David"* (Matt. 21: 9, 15), thereby acknowledging their belief that Jesus is the coming King described by the Prophet Zechariah. And though this is a few days away from the start of Passover, the waving of the palm branches, usually associated with the Feast of Tabernacles, is done to underscore their belief that Jesus is the Messiah and true King of Israel.

However, the people's response to His entry into Jerusalem shows they do not understand that His kingdom will come in a very different way than expected. His subsequent weeping over Jerusalem will cut to the heart of His purpose for coming this first time. The Savior mourns over the spiritual state of His chosen people,

> *O Jerusalem, Jerusalem, the city that kills the prophets and stones those sent to her! How often I wanted to gather your children together, just as a hen gathers her brood under her wings, and you would not have it! Behold, your house is left to you desolate; and I say to you, you will not see Me until the time comes when you say, "Blessed is He who comes in the name of the Lord!"* (Luke 13:34–35)

The Jewish people think they are getting a king who will vanquish the Romans the way the Maccabees vanquished the Seleucid king Antiochus IV (reigned 175–164 B.C.). Instead, Jesus enters Jerusalem on the day the lamb is selected and presents Himself as the perfect, spotless Lamb of God.

TEMPTED IN ALL THINGS . . . YET WITHOUT SIN

Just as the first Passover lamb is brought into each household, each community, to be examined to make sure it is perfect and without blemish, Jesus enters the household of Israel and allows Himself to be examined for four days to show that He is a spotless and unblemished lamb. The religious leaders question the authority of His teaching. The chief priests and elders of the people come to him and ask,

> *By what authority are You doing these things, and who gave You this authority?* (Matt. 21:23)

His response stuns the Jewish leaders:

> *I will also ask you one thing, which if you tell Me, I will also tell you by what authority I do these things. The baptism of John was from what source, from heaven or from men?* (Matt. 21:24–25)

The leaders do not answer the question as they are afraid of how the people will react if they do. And as He promised, Jesus does not answer their question about the nature of His authority.

The next question, asked by the Pharisees and the Herodians, involves the role of government. The Pharisees are the purists and separatists, not wanting Rome to be involved in Jewish religious questions. The Herodians are supportive of Herod and Roman rule and thereby are hated by most Jews. Yet these strange bedfellows approach Jesus together and ask a question:

> Tell us then, what do You think? Is it lawful to give a poll-tax to Caesar, or not? (Matt. 22:17)

They test Jesus to see if He will acknowledge Roman authority or encourage rebellion. Again, His answer disarms them.

> But Jesus perceived their malice, and said, "Why are you testing Me, you hypocrites? Show Me the coin used for the poll-tax." And they brought Him a denarius. And He said to them, "Whose likeness and inscription is this?" They said to Him, "Caesar's." Then He said to them, "Then render to Caesar the things that are Caesar's; and to God the things that are God's." And hearing this, they were amazed, and leaving Him, they went away. (Matt. 22:18–22)

The Sadducees, the high priestly caste who also do not believe in the resurrection, ask a third question. Their question seems to be designed to show that Jesus' knowledge of Scripture is inferior to theirs. They ask about a possible Levirate marriage that suddenly ends when the man dies, and so his name and property rights continue on through his brother, who dutifully marries the widow and becomes a father to his dead brother's children. However, in this unusual case concocted by the Sadducees, there are seven brothers, none of whom father any children, and they and finally the widow all eventually die. The question they then ask is designed to stump even Jesus:

> *In the resurrection, therefore, whose wife of the seven will she be? For they all had married her.* (Matt. 22:28)

The question drips with sarcasm, and they are sure that Jesus will stumble and be unable to answer, proving He is not the Messiah. Jesus' response overwhelms them. He says,

> *You are mistaken, not understanding the Scriptures nor the power of God. For in the resurrection they neither marry nor are given in marriage, but are like angels in heaven. But regarding the resurrection of the dead, have you not read what was spoken to you by God: "I am the God of Abraham, and the God of Isaac, and the God of Jacob"? He is not the God of the dead but of the living. When the crowds heard this, they were astonished at His teaching.* (Matt. 22:29–33)

Jesus passes all the tests and shows Himself to be pure, spotless, and without sin.

Later, even the pagan Pontius Pilate, the Roman governor and political head of the community, will declare that Jesus is without blemish. After examining him, he will say, *"I find no guilt in this man"* (Luke 23:4). The Lamb is indeed worthy to be slain.

After completing this period of testing during the first four days of the week, the time for Yeshua's final Passover meal with His disciples has come. This is the apex of His ministry and the beginning of what many think will be the end of His ministry. At last it is Thursday, the fourteenth of Nisan, and Yeshua and the Twelve recline at the table and celebrate Passover. During the meal Jesus tells His disciples that there is a betrayer among them. He warns them with an announcement: *"Truly, truly, I say to you, that one of you will betray Me"* (John 13:21). The disciples are shocked and cannot believe this is possible. Prompted by Peter, John asks Jesus who it is, and Jesus responds, *"That is the one for whom I shall dip the morsel and give it to him"* (v. 26). Jesus then dips the matzah in what some have suggested was the bitter herbs placed on the Passover table and offers it to Judas, who takes it from Jesus, acknowledging he will indeed be the betrayer. Satan then takes possession of Judas and the betrayal process begins that will lead to Jesus' brutal death foreshadowed in the death of the perfect lamb at that first Passover in Egypt.

Worthy Is the Lamb That Was Slain

Jesus is the Lamb of God who takes away the sin of the world. He is the fulfillment of Passover. Like the first Passover lambs sacrificed to redeem Israel from slavery in Egypt, Jesus' death on the cross redeems us from slavery to sin. Reflecting on all of this, the Apostle Paul says, *"Christ our Passover also has been sacrificed"* (1 Cor. 5:7), and just as the first Passover was very personal and the Israelites personally applied the blood of the lambs to the doors of their houses, we too, by faith, need to personally apply the blood of Jesus, the Lamb of God, to the doors of our hearts. Have you made Passover personal? If you haven't, I pray that you will, perhaps this Passover.

3

Passover Lessons
for Your Children

Rachel Goldstein-Davis

The children are the most important observers of the Passover Seder! We hope you will find this chapter useful in engaging the children to celebrate the Seder and to understand the Gospel truths woven throughout this great celebration.

Why Teach Children about the Passover?

It is important to teach the Bible to our children, as it says in Deuteronomy 6:6,

> *"You shall teach them [the commandments] diligently to your children, and shall talk of them when you sit in your house, and when you walk by the way, and when you lie down, and when you rise"* (ESV).

We spend a lot of time praying for our children and helping them draw close to Jesus, whose Hebrew name is Yeshua. We want them to walk closely with their Messiah and we know that their spiritual lives are best shaped when they are young.

We teach them stories from the Old and New Testaments, but many times we might not fully understand some of the backgrounds of the stories ourselves. That's because both the Old and New Testaments were written by people whose cultures were far different than ours is today. There is great value in teaching our children God's truth from the Old Testament, as it is especially picturesque and filled with physical illustrations of spiritual truths. But to teach the Old Testament we first need to put ourselves in that ancient culture's "sandals," and then create lessons that can be understood in our modern age.

One Old Testament story that's especially important to teach is the Passover. This magnificent story paints a portrait of redemption that became a reference point for all future stories of national and spiritual liberation in the Scriptures and points beautifully to the ultimate story of salvation in Jesus, *"the Lamb of God who takes away the sin of the world!"* (John 1:29).

Every year Jewish people across the globe gather in homes to celebrate the Passover Seder and remember how the Lord won their ancestors' freedom from bondage; miraculously sustained them in the desert with food, water, and shelter; and taught them to rely utterly on Him. They celebrate how He brought their forefathers back to the Promised Land of Israel. There are so many wonderful lessons embedded in the Passover that enable us to impact the young lives God has called us to mold and develop.

Most importantly, we can use the Passover to teach our children about the glorious salvation we have received through Jesus the Messiah. There are so many parallels between the Gospel story and the ancient Passover as well as the way the holiday has been observed by Jewish people throughout the centuries.

For example, in the story of the Exodus from Egypt the Lord passed over the homes of the Israelites whose doors were smeared with the blood of the perfect and innocent sacrificial lamb and did not slay the firstborn males in each of the homes. We understand that this was a prophetic type of what was to come as God has also forgiven and passed over all whose hearts are covered by the blood of Yeshua, the Lamb of God, and have received Him as their Savior and Lord. And just as the Israelites of old were freed from bondage, those who have trusted in Yeshua are freed from bondage to sin.

We do not need to wander in the wilderness of this life and in a world that is passing away. The Lord through His Word and His Spirit has given us redemption, hope, and direction to live for Him. We are not simply wandering through this life but instead are becoming more and more like our Messiah each day until He comes again. We have a purpose in life that goes beyond our everyday concern for survival. He is our joy and salvation and provides for all of our needs. We understand that redeemed people still struggle, but the Lord is faithful. These are lessons our children need to understand, and the Passover story provides us with excellent teaching tools. But, of course, there is much more! The Passover helps our kids understand that the Lord, who is great and mighty, cares for even the smallest details in our lives.

Through interacting with the items on the Seder table, our children are able to handle, see, and experience the message of redemption Jewish people have been retelling for centuries. We are also able to introduce our children to the story of the Last Supper observed by Jesus and His disciples, which was most likely an earlier version of the Passover Seder related to the modern version that has developed since the destruction of the Temple in 70 A.D.

By understanding the parallels between the traditions of the Jewish Passover Seder and the Last Supper, our children will gain a perspective on their own salvation that is richer and deeper and more understandable because the Seder is so very visual and tactile.

Passover in Israel and in Jewish communities throughout the world is a major undertaking and requires a great deal of work and preparation. All foods must be bought days ahead as the family usually gathers from all over for what is by far the largest family get-together of the year. Although many Jewish homes are secular, Passover is still celebrated by more than 80 percent of Jewish households, and in Israel that number is probably closer to 100 percent! Jewish people know the Passover story, and it is one of the experiences that draws Jewish people together across countries, nationalities, and languages.

The Passover provides a perfect point of commonality between Jewish people and Christians. Jewish people simply do not understand the ultimate fulfillment of the holiday through Jesus the Messiah. It is our responsibility as believers in Yeshua to share this story with our Jewish loved ones and friends. It is also an opportunity for our children to speak to their young friends about their faith in Jesus.

Your children probably have Jewish friends in school, extended families, the playground, etc. They can wish their Jewish friends a "Happy Passover!" and speak with them about their upcoming Seder, if they know something about Passover and how the Jewish festival ties into their own faith in Jesus. These simple conversations about the Lord can be used by God as a small seed planted in the lives of Jewish children when they are young. We believe it is not appropriate for adults to take these initiatives in talking with children without the Jewish parents' permission. But we believe it is appropriate for your children to swap stories about their culture and faith.

GOALS FOR THESE LESSONS

The goals for the following three lessons are (1) to teach your children about Passover and its fulfillment in Jesus through the retelling of the Bible's story of Passover, (2) to show your children how Jewish people celebrate Passover, and (3) to educate your children about Jewish people through playing games, learning Hebrew words, doing crafts and eating some of the Passover elements. Depending on your time, you might decide to do the complete lesson or pick and choose parts. At least the option is available. You will find a helpful summary of the story at the beginning of every lesson.

We hope and pray you will find the lessons to be helpful and that your children will be blessed through understanding the Jewish backgrounds of the Last Supper and gain a better understanding of our salvation through Jesus, the Lamb of God.

LESSON 1: Preparing for Passover

Retelling: The Story of Moses and the Israelites in Egypt

More than 2,500 years ago, Joseph and his family moved to Egypt to escape a famine in the land of Canaan, which was later called Israel. They survived, and the generations of their family grew until they became a very large group of people. Pharaoh, the ruler of Egypt, became afraid of all the Hebrews, as the Jewish people at that time were called, living in his country, so he made them slaves. He even made a law that when Hebrew babies were born, the boys should be killed.

A baby boy named Moses was born and his mother wanted to save him, so she put him in a waterproof basket and put the basket in the Nile River. Pharaoh's daughter found the baby and adopted him, and he was raised in Pharaoh's palace.

When Moses grew up, he became very upset about how his people, the Israelites, were being treated. When he saw a Hebrew slave being beaten by an Egyptian taskmaster, Moses killed the Egyptian. This was a horrible thing, and Moses fled to the desert in fear. While Moses was in the desert, in the land of Midian, God spoke to him from a burning bush that would not burn up. God told him to go back to Egypt and tell Pharaoh, *"Let my people go!"* (Exod. 9:1)

Moses asked Pharaoh many times to let the people of Israel go free, but even after nine plagues fell on Egypt, Pharaoh's heart was still hard and he would not agree. The final plague was the scariest—the destroyer, sometimes referred to as the "angel of death," was going to kill all the firstborn males in Egypt.

The Lord told Moses to warn his people to carefully listen and obey in order to save their lives. They had to clean their houses and get rid of all *chametz* (KHUH-mitz).

Chametz is yeast, or leaven—so they had to throw out all their bread and cookies. They had to bake *matzah* (MAHTZ-uh), which is bread made without yeast that's more like crackers than bread, and they had to kill a little lamb. The lamb was to be perfect, with no spots or bruises and no broken bones. The people had to take some blood from the lamb and put it on the doorposts and lintel (doorframe) of their houses so that the destroyer would "pass over" their home. The lamb was to be roasted and eaten with bitter herbs and matzah, and the people had no time to relax. They had to be packed and ready to leave— with their shoes and jackets on.

That night, the destroyer came and killed all the firstborn sons in Egypt—except those in families that had obeyed God's instructions to put the lamb's blood on their doors. There was much crying in Egypt that night, and Pharaoh's own son died. Finally, after this horrible thing, Pharaoh told the Jewish people they were free to go.

Main Points

1. The Israelites were slaves in Egypt, and they wanted to be free so they could go and live in the Promised Land.

2. Moses kept asking Pharaoh to let the people go and Pharaoh said no, even after nine plagues.

3. The people prepared for the Passover night by getting rid of *chametz* (leaven or yeast). The New Testament says that leaven or yeast represents sin in our lives (read 1 Corinthians 5:7–8). Yeast is the ingredient that makes bread puffy. We don't want to be "puffed up" with pride, making fun of other people and thinking we are better than them.

4. Just like the lamb that was sacrificed had to be perfect, Jesus (who is called the Lamb of God) was also perfect

and sinless. The blood of the Passover lamb saved the people from death in Egypt, and Jesus' blood saves us from eternal death and gives us eternal life!

Craft

Make two batches of dough—one with leaven (yeast) and one without—so that the children can see the difference between risen dough and flat dough. You can make flat dough right in front of the children, getting their help too, but you might need to make risen dough at home so that it has hours to rise. You can also bring in a box of store-bought matzah for the kids to eat.

Hebrew Words

Seder (SAY-der). The Jewish ceremonial dinner on the first night of Passover, with lots of Bible reading and eating traditional foods.

matzah (MAHTZ-uh). A hard cracker-like bread made from only flour and water (taste it).

chametz (KHUH-mitz). Leaven or yeast, or all food that has this ingredient.

Bible Verse

1 Corinthians 5:7–8

Game: Search for the Chametz

Hide bagels, muffins, bread, cereal, or cookies all over the room for the kids to find. These could be plastic food items (like toys or magnets) or the real thing (which they will be quite happy about). If the food is real, make sure to seal the items in plastic bags to prevent a crumbly mess and in case some are not found.

LESSON 2: THE PLAGUES OF PASSOVER

Retelling: The Story of Pharaoh and the Ten Plagues

Pharaoh was the ruler of his country; he was boss over everyone in Egypt. Suddenly, Moses came and demanded that the Israelites—Pharaoh's slaves—all leave Egypt. Pharaoh had gotten used to having this free labor. He was building a huge kingdom and needed them to make himself great, so when Moses delivered God's message, "Let my people go!" Pharaoh would not listen to Moses. God sent plague after plague on Egypt, but Pharaoh was stubborn and would not change his mind.

Each plague that fell on Egypt represented a battle between our God and the Egyptian gods. The Egyptians had "gods" for everything—water, crops, livestock, health—so each plague was directed towards these areas on purpose to show that the Egyptian gods were false gods. Our God is mighty and powerful, and the plagues that fell on Egypt are an example of His strength.

During the first nine plagues, Pharaoh would not listen and did not want to admit that he had lost against the Most High God. The tenth plague—the death of all the firstborn males in Egypt—was the harshest. Finally, Pharaoh agreed to let the Israelites go, but not before his people and the land of Egypt had suffered dire consequences.

Main Point

God wants us to pay close attention to Him. How many times does God try to get our attention and we are stubborn, or we think our ideas are better than His? Still, He keeps trying to get us to listen and obey Him. He gives us chances and is patient with us. How many times will it take?

Theme Words / Bible Passages / Object Lessons

This lesson can be as interactive as you wish. Start by asking the children to list the plagues; chances are that they will forget one or two. Give them the word for each plague (blood, frogs, gnats, etc.). Ask them what they think it was like to live through the plagues. Maybe they have experienced something similar (hail, tornados, hurricanes, heavy floods). How did they react? You could also reenact the plagues—this will take some props and preparation on your part.

1. ***The Plague of Blood*** (Exod. 7:14–24). All the water in Egypt was turned to blood. It was disgusting; it stank and the fish died. In a hot, desert country, the people needed fresh water to drink and water their crops!

   OBJECT LESSON: If you want to be creative, have a clear pitcher with inconspicuous red dye on the bottom (maybe place the pitcher on a dark table mat or piece of paper to hide the dye). Fill the pitcher with clear water and let the children watch it turn to "blood."

2. ***The Plague of Frogs*** (Exod. 7:25–8:15). There were frogs everywhere! Have the children imagine all the places where the frogs would be! Once the plague was over, all the frogs died and stank— pretty gross.

   OBJECT LESSON: If the children want to be silly—have them hop around like frogs!

3. ***The Plague of Gnats*** (Exod. 8:16–19). These tiny bugs were everywhere: on the ground, in the homes, even on people's skin!

OBJECT LESSON: Suddenly throw some store-bought plastic bugs on the kids next to you. It should get a reaction!

4. **The Plague of Flies** (Exod. 8:20–32). Do you know the song "Shoo fly, don't bother me"? Imagine swarms and swarms of flies hovering everywhere, touching you, covering the ground, in your food, on your pets—so annoying and disgusting. However, there were no insects bothering the Israelites where they were living.

OBJECT LESSON: Pretend to gulp the imaginary flies around you. "Oops, I think I swallowed a fly!"

5. **Plague of Pestilence** (Exod. 9:1–7). In those days, they didn't have cars or tractors to pull heavy things around; instead they had horses, camels, and strong cattle. All these animals died. How were they to get milk and meat? How were they going to eat, to work . . . and what happened if you had a favorite goat? The Israelites' livestock did not die. Pharaoh knew this, but it only made him more stubborn.

6. **The Plague of Boils** (Exod. 9:8–12). Have you ever had the chicken pox, or better yet, a really big red zit? That is kind of what boils are. The Egyptians and their animals had them everywhere on their bodies and it hurt to touch, to sleep, to move.

OBJECT LESSON: Have the children pretend to scratch like they have the worst chicken pox in the world!

7. **The Plague of Hail** (Exod. 9:13–35). The Lord sent the worst hailstorm ever; Egypt had never seen a storm like this! Remember that in a desert climate like Egypt's, they might never have seen ice or

snow! The hailstones were so big that they destroyed everything, and anyone who was left outside died—both people and animals. The hail destroyed most of the crops, too. But God was merciful and gave the message to Pharaoh with enough time to tell the people to bring everything under shelter. There was thunder and hail and fire that ran down to the earth. But where the children of Israel were living there was no hail. Pharaoh almost listened to God and let the people go, but after the terrifying storm was over, he changed his mind.

OBJECT LESSON: In the middle of your explanation, throw cotton balls, ping pong balls, or marshmallows on the kids.

8. *The Plague of Locusts* (Exod. 10:1–20). Pharaoh tried to make a deal with God by allowing the men to leave Egypt but making the women and children stay. This was not acceptable, and God sent another devastating plague to teach Pharaoh to listen. There had already been frogs, gnats/lice, and flies to swarm around everything, and then hail to destroy the crops. Now locusts came to eat up the last bits of grass, leaves, and fruit. They were so numerous that the ground was completely covered by them!

9. *The Plague of Darkness* (Exod. 10:21–29). Pharaoh tried to make another deal with God, saying that the people could leave, but their cattle had to stay. Moses reminded Pharaoh that everything must leave Egypt—even all the Israelites' possessions. It was all or nothing! Pharaoh got angry and told Moses never to come before him again. The Lord then sent complete darkness on Egypt for

three days. But the children of Israel had light in their homes.

> OBJECT LESSON: Have you ever been in a dark cave where you can't even see your hand in front of you? In darkness, you get disoriented, you can't get anything done; it's boring and scary! If you can, turn off the lights and sit in darkness for a few minutes. Maybe retell this part of the story in darkness (or with the kids' eyes closed).

10. **Death of the Firstborn** (Exod. 11:1–10). (Don't worry, we won't reenact this one!) It would have been better if the Egyptians had recognized God's power over the natural and spiritual elements of the world.

Instead, the destroyer passed through Egypt and wherever the blood of the spotless lamb was not seen on the doors of the homes, the firstborn males died—both human and animal. During this horrible night, the Israelites had very important instructions from God in order to save their lives and prepare them for leaving Egypt. They obeyed God and were ready to go with everything packed, and as they ate their Passover dinner they knew they were saved from the destroyer as he passed over them. That night, even Pharaoh's own son died.

After these ten plagues, Pharaoh at last let the Israelites leave Egypt. It took ten plagues for Pharaoh to finally obey God. How many times does it take for us to listen to God and do what He says? It's best if it's just one time!

Craft

Ask the kids which of the first nine plagues would have bothered them the most. Invite them to draw a picture about one of the plagues.

LESSON 3:
Participating in the Passover Seder

This lesson focuses on the actual Passover Seder. There is some preparation you can do beforehand, and some you can do with the children. The Seder elements are listed below, and after the kids have decorated their Seder plates you can eat them all together and discuss their meanings.

If you would like a Chosen People Ministries staff person to present the Passover Seder to your Sunday school class, home school group, or your church family, contact our Church Ministries staff (www.chosenpeople.com/church), who would be happy to speak with you or your pastor.

Main Point

It is God who saves us. He wants us to remember what He has done for us so we will trust in Him.

Bible Passage

Exodus 12

Retelling / Craft / Hebrew Words

Let's have a Seder!

Buy some large throwaway paper plates and child-safe markers. Each child can draw five circles on his or her plate and write the names of the items (given below) in transliterated Hebrew and/or English.

Now you get to participate in your own Seder! We will go through each Seder item and explain what it means, so you can see, smell, and taste them and learn more about God and His Messiah in the Passover meal. Some of these items are biblical and some are traditional. The biblical items that Moses and the Israelites used are found in Exodus 12 and are the most important—matzah (unleavened bread), maror (bitter herbs) and zeroah (lamb shankbone)—while the other items have been added over the years by Jewish rabbis from around the world for families to use to help them celebrate the Passover.

You will want to try to find some matzah, the unleavened bread representing a life without sin. The Jewish people had to bake this bread quickly, without allowing the dough time to rise, because they ate their dinner with their jackets and shoes on—ready to leave Egypt at any moment as soon as Moses said, "Go!" How different it is now. As you participate in your Seder so many years after the first Passover, we use the best dishes, take our time, and eat like kings and queens in freedom!

The Cup of Blessing (or ***The Cup of Sanctification***). Take a sip of grape juice. We begin the Seder by saying,

> Blessed are You, Lord our God, King of the Universe, who created the fruit of the vine.

Passover Items on the Seder Plate

Using the Seder plate that the kids made with the five circles, put all the items on the plate in their correct positions before starting the Seder.

1. ***Zeroah*** (zeh-ROH-ah). Lamb shankbone. The bone reminds us of the Passover lamb sacrificed for the first Passover. Jesus is our Passover Lamb who died to give us eternal life! Jewish people don't understand that Jesus is the Lamb of God, so let's take a moment to pray for them. Put this item in the top right hand circle on your plate—at the 2:00 PM position on a clock.

2. ***Charoset*** (khah-ROH-set). A mixture of finely chopped apples (turned brown), honey, nuts (do

not include if there are allergies), cinnamon, and a dash of grape juice—very tasty! This mixture looks like mortar for bricks. When the Israelites were slaves, they had to mix straw, dirt, and water to make their own mortar for building. The charoset reminds us of the hard slave work in Egypt. But why does a reminder of something so bitter taste so sweet? Because we remember that even in hard work and suffering, we can have redemption. The Israelites were freed and were able to go to the Promised Land! We can remember that our lives can be sweet and wonderful with Jesus! Put this item in the bottom right circle on the plate—at the 4:00 PM position on a clock. Enjoy eating some charoset spread on pieces of matzah crackers.

3. **Maror** (mah-ROAR). Horseradish root (from a jar—the red kind is not as spicy as the white kind. It is wise to taste only a dip first, as it might be too spicy for some!). This bitter herb represents the harsh suffering and bitter times the Jewish people endured when they were slaves in Egypt. Put this item in the middle of the plate. Spread a little on pieces of matzah and eat.

4. **Karpas** (CAR-pahs). Parsley (just a sprig or two). The parsley is a symbol of spring and new life— just as new leaves grow on trees in the spring! It reminds us of the rebirth of the Jewish nation and of freedom. Put this item in the bottom left circle on the plate—at the 8:00 PM position on a clock. Break off a sprig, dip it in salt water, and eat it. Life was hard for the Israelites and even though there was the season of spring and new life, there were also many salty tears.

Cups or small bowls of salt water are placed on the table (not on the Seder plate) and are meant for dipping the parsley and egg pieces. Salt water represents tears. As the Israelites yearned to be freed from slavery and go to live in the Promised Land, they shed tears of sorrow. Thankfully, we can rejoice as believers in Jesus, because we have been given the ultimate gift anyone could receive—eternal life with Him!

5. *Beitzah* (bay-TZAH). Hard-boiled egg (this can be cut up and each child can be given a half or a quarter). This reminds us of the ceremonial offering that was brought to the Temple each Passover. Also, since Passover always falls in the spring, the egg reminds us of life—new life in Jesus. Put this item in the 10:00 PM position on a clock. Also, take a piece of your egg and dip it into the salt water. New life was immersed in tears when the Israelites were slaves.

Charoset and Maror Sandwich. Put a bit of the horseradish and the sweet apple mixture between two pieces of matzah and eat the "sandwich." These two ingredients together stand for the joy and sorrow that was found in the Israelites' lives when they were in Egypt: they were slaves (which was bitter) and then were granted freedom (which was sweet). Even though bad things sometimes happen in our lives, we have the sweetness of knowing that Jesus set us free from being slaves to sin.

The Cup of Plagues (or *The Cup of Judgment*). Have the children dip a finger in their cup and make a dot of grape juice on their plate for each of the ten plagues (they can make designs like smiley faces or rainbows on their plate). Recite the plagues together while doing so.

Matzah Tash (MAHTZ-uh TAHSH). A matzah bag with three compartments. If you don't have one, you can take a large white napkin or a large white cloth and fold it into three sections. Place a piece of matzah in each section. Then remove the middle matzah, break it in two, and put half back. The remaining piece is now named the *afikoman* (ah-fee-KO-men), a Greek word meaning "that which is to come after." The afikoman is wrapped in white linen and hidden. Have all the kids close their eyes for a minute. Hide the afikoman and ask the kids to get up and look for it. Tell them the child who finds it should bring it back. When this happens, unwrap the afikoman, break it in pieces and distribute to all the participants.

You might pause for a moment and ask, "Does anyone know why the matzah tash and the hidden matzah are important?" Then explain that some rabbis described the three compartments as representing the Patriarchs: Abraham, Isaac, and Jacob; and others said they stood for the divisions of the people of Israel: the priests, the Levites, and the Jewish people in general. As believers in the Messiah, we might look at the three pieces as representing the triune nature of God: the Father, the Son, and the Holy Spirit, although we realize that Jewish people do not traditionally believe in the Trinity.

Did you notice that the middle piece of matzah was broken, and the afikoman part was wrapped in a napkin and hidden? The rabbis aren't sure why this custom started. We believe this might represent the piece of matzah Jesus broke and handed to His disciples at the Last Supper. We read in the Gospel of Luke,

> *And when He had taken some bread and given thanks, He broke it and gave it to them, saying, "This is My body which is given for you; do this in remembrance of Me."* (Luke 22:19)

Understanding the traditions of the afikoman gives us a better understanding of the Lord's Supper, since on the very next day Jesus would be crucified, wrapped for burial (hidden), and three days later raised from the dead (1 Cor. 15:3–4). We now understand that Jesus may have intended the breaking of the matzah at the Last Supper as a prophecy of His death, burial, and resurrection. We are sure the disciples did not fully understand this until after these events happened, but as followers of Jesus and upon reflection, we can see it. *Eat your piece of afikoman matzah.*

The Cup of Redemption. Jesus next took the cup that is sipped after the meal. This is associated with the third cup of the Passover, the cup called Redemption. It reminds us of the shed blood of the little lamb slain for the redemption of the firstborn male of the Israelite homes in Egypt. This event, of course, led to the Exodus. In the Gospel of Luke we read,

> *And in the same way He took the cup after they had eaten, saying, "This cup which is poured out for you is the new covenant in My blood."* (Luke 22:20)

Once again we see that Jesus was speaking about Himself, since the next day His blood would be shed for the forgiveness of sin. The cup Jewish people sipped for centuries pointed to the death of the Lamb of God who was sacrificed for the sins of us all. We celebrate the fulfillment of this salvation when we take the cup of juice at the Lord's Table for Communion or the Lord's Supper. *Drink a little cup of grape juice.*

The Cup of Praise (or ***The Cup of Rejoicing***). We drink the fourth cup to express the joy we have as a people because of God's glorious act of redemption on our behalf. He saved our sons through the shed blood of the lamb in the original Exodus and as followers of Yeshua and those who understand that the third cup was fulfilled at the Lord's Supper with the cup Jesus used to remind us that ultimate redemption comes through His shed blood for our sins. This gives us a greater reason to rejoice, and we drink the fourth cup and praise God for the salvation available to both Jews and Gentiles through the Lamb of God who takes away the sin of the world.

A *song* is sung at the end of every Seder: *L'Shana HaBa'ah B'Yerushalayim!* "Next Year in Jerusalem!" This wonderful and lively song speaks of the future day of Messianic redemption when the Messiah will come and bring the Jewish people back to the Land of Israel to celebrate the Passover. Of course, as believers in Jesus, we believe He has come once and is coming again. What a wonderful opportunity we have now to tell our Jewish friends that the Messiah has come and His name is Yeshua—*"the Lamb of God who takes away the sin of the world!"* (John 1:29).

PASSOVER AROUND THE WORLD

Games and Songs

Every child loves the Passover Seder. It is meant for kids and has many object lessons and hands-on experiences. The parents involve the kids, as it is a long meal and they might get restless. Songs, games, and great memories can be had by all. One game, just mentioned, is the hiding and finding of the afikoman. Although hidden for part of the meal, the afikoman is still integral to the Seder and it helps to communicate a powerful message. Usually, the child who finds it can barter for its return, knowing how important it is to the Seder. Money, tickets to fun events, and special meals are all great rewards for the one who finds the afikoman.

At the start of the Seder, a final, thorough search for chametz is traditionally made in the home. Often, the father hides some crumbs in a corner for a child to find. The crumbs are scooped up in a dust pan or newspaper. In some places and/or eras, these last crumbs of leaven were taken outside to a communal bonfire and thrown in, burning the last "sin" found in the home.

Also, it's the job of the youngest child at the Seder who is able to recite special questions (traditionally in Hebrew), including "Why is this night different than all other nights?" and "Why do we eat all these different foods?" It's a rite of passage for the youngest and takes many days and weeks to practice (and to get over the nerves and embarrassment of public speaking), but every child does it.

The point of the Seder is to keep the kids engaged, asking questions, learning, and interacting. You can even play Passover Bingo, A Moses Basket full of Questions and Answers, Eye Spy, as well as make clay models of Passover items. Suggestions for such games and family activities can readily be found online. Getting ready for Passover can be a stressful time, but playing some games or doing special activities can make it fun for everyone!

Every Seder has many songs that can be sung to many different tunes and melodies. It seems like each country and culture has its own way to sing these traditional songs. Many are in Hebrew and take a while to learn, but some notable ones are *L'Shanah HaBa'ah, Dayenu, Echad Mi Yodeah*, and *Eliyahu HaNavi*.[5]

Everyone remembers Mom's brisket on Passover, but not everyone might want to eat the bitter herbs. Jewish

---

5   For these and other Passover songs (titles spelled in various ways), see this book's website for additional Passover-themed resources: www.messiahinthepassover.com. There are also Passover karaoke apps that will play songs on your phone or mobile device.

children will remember the double-daring done to see who would eat the biggest bite of horseradish (maror) and subsequently turn red, choke a little, and have tears streaming down their faces after the flush simmered down a little. Each country prepares the *gefilte* fish (traditional appetizer) a little differently, and most children will poke it with their fork to see if it wiggles back. Everyone loves the *charoset* (be mindful of the nuts in the recipe if anyone has food allergies), the grape juice, and the special Passover desserts. This is what Passover fun is all about—the feasting on food!

TO REMEMBER ESPECIALLY

Passover is a wonderful holiday that helps bond us with our Jewish brothers and sisters who are celebrating the feast around the world. It will break down walls of suspicion when you, too, understand this festival and can genuinely wish your Jewish friends "Happy Passover!" It helps us more fully comprehend the message of redemption in both the Old and New Testament and especially gives us new insight into the words of Jesus. The Passover will help the children appreciate the Lord's Supper or Communion in a new and deeper way.

Teaching kids about celebrating Passover takes some preparation and study, but the rewards are immense. Each element is an object lesson of redemption, joy, tears, offerings, life, freedom, prophecy, faithfulness, and conquering death! We could dwell on these words for weeks!

It is fun to teach the kids some Hebrew words and Jewish customs and to introduce them to new foods. It will help them better understand their physical and/or spiritual Jewish heritage (Rom. 11:17–21) and even create opportunities for them to witness to their friends. Making a fun and interactive Seder will be well worth the effort—for kids and adults, too!

Praying with Children to Accept Jesus through the Passover

During these lessons and especially during the Seder, there will be opportunities to ask the children how they feel about what they are learning and if they have questions. As you prepare to discuss salvation with your child, here are a few things to keep in mind. First, spend time in prayer asking:

- that the Holy Spirit would prepare your child.
- that He would help you present the information clearly.
- that He would give your child understanding.
- that He would convince your child of the truth of your words.

We recommend that you talk with each child alone and don't rush through it. Use simple words your child will understand and explain phrases that might confuse him or her (like "invite Jesus into your heart"). At the end, ask questions to make sure your child understands all that you have said.

Don't push your children to make a decision. Your children's salvation is a matter between them and the Holy Spirit. The Holy Spirit must be the one who convinces them of their sin and need for salvation. As a result, you may need to revisit the conversation with your children several times. At the right time the Holy Spirit will speak to them.

You can ask the children what part of the Passover lesson really impacted them. It might be the matzah—how it represents purity and is not puffed up. It might be how God protects and cares for us and provides for all our needs. It might be the afikoman—how it is wrapped in linen, hidden, and brought back—just as Jesus died, was buried, and raised from the dead. It might be how the Passover lamb had to be perfect, without blemish, and its blood was put on the people's doors—just as Jesus, the Lamb of God, was perfect and sinless and His blood is put on the doors of our hearts when we give our hearts to Him. It might simply be the dipping of the parsley (life) in salt water (tears). You never know what might touch a child's heart and understanding.

You can spend time with your children and discuss these amazing points about the Lord and our salvation, and pray together. Take some time to pray, confess sin, acknowledge that Jesus is our Messiah and that He died to give us the gift of eternal life. He died willingly for us, and will take on all our sin and shame. We can have joy forever, knowing that if we belong to Him, we will live with Him for eternity. In the meantime, we are on earth to share His joy and glory and love with others, to proclaim His message and tell others of their Messiah.

For additional information you might review any number of Jewish websites on the topic of Passover.[6] And of course, this book will provide you with all the background you need to teach the children about this glorious festival.

6   For additional resources, see the series of brief Passover-themed articles at "Passover," BBC, last updated July 9, 2009, www.bbc.co.uk/religion/religions/judaism/holydays/passover_1.shtml. Also see this book's website for additional Passover-themed resources: www.messiahinthepassover.com.

4

THE GOSPEL
IN THE PASSOVER SEDER

LARRY FELDMAN

Passover is the story of redemption. It reveals how God
redeemed our people, the Israelites, from the bondage of
slavery in Egypt and also delivered "a mixed multitude,"
perhaps including some Egyptians who chose to identify
with the God of Abraham, Isaac, and Jacob (Exod.
12:38). Any and all who acted in faith and obeyed God's
instructions given through Moses experienced God's
deliverance from His judgment on Egypt.

It is likely that those who offered the lamb originally did
not fully comprehend the significance of sacrificing an
animal, shedding its blood, and then placing that lamb's
blood on the two doorposts and lintel of the house in
which they were to eat it (Exod. 12:7). From our vantage
point, we recognize that this sacrifice foreshadows the
death of the Messiah, Yeshua (Jesus), the Lamb of God
who takes away the sin of the world for both Jewish and
Gentile people. For everyone who believes and receives
Yeshua as their atonement, it is as if, by faith in His
atoning sacrifice, they personally put His blood over the

doorposts and lintel of their lives and are redeemed from the bondage of sin and death.

The Passover *Seder*, a Hebrew word that means "order" or "service," refers to the ancient ceremonial meal that has become the primary means of celebrating the Passover today.. The Passover Seder proclaims the message of salvation for all people, and each aspect of the ceremonial meal can be used to proclaim the good news of Messiah Yeshua. It makes sense, therefore, that we examine in this chapter the many elements of the Seder, some directly from Scripture and some introduced by Jewish tradition over the years, which point to redemption through Messiah Yeshua's death and resurrection. We will focus on how various aspects and elements of the Passover Seder can be explained to your Jewish friends and family that by faith they might see with hearts unveiled the glory of Messiah in the Passover (2 Cor. 3:12–18).[7]

SHARING THE GOOD NEWS THROUGH THE *KARPAS* (DIPPING OF THE PARSLEY)

The Passover ceremony revolves around a plate (called a Seder plate) with various elements placed on it to remind us of the key aspects of Passover. One such element is green parsley. After initiating the Passover Seder by drinking the first cup of the fruit of the vine, the ceremony continues with the dipping of the parsley (Hebrew, *karpas*). The leader of the Seder, generally the father in the home, asks everyone to take a sprig of the herb and hold it up as he explains its significance. He begins by stating the obvious, that the *karpas* is green. The

---

7   For more on how the Passover Seder can be used to explain the truths of the Gospel to Jewish as well as non-Jewish friends, see chapter 1, "Passover in Your Home," by Cathy Wilson, and chapter 5, "A Messianic Family Haggadah," by the Staff of Chosen People Ministries.

color is supposed to remind everyone that in springtime, during the first months of the Hebrew calendar, God's mighty arm brought the people of Israel forth from slavery in Egypt to freedom.

He then goes on to explain that the karpas is dipped twice in salt water. The first time is to remind us that we were redeemed from the bitterness of slavery and many tears. The second time reminds us that we were brought forth through the Red Sea, which God parted for us but closed over the Egyptians. The Red Sea is also salty and so this second dipping once more reminds us of God's deliverance.

The most significant part of this ceremony is understanding the reason why we dip at all. The explanation is found in the Bible, in the book of Exodus:

> *Then Moses called for all the elders of Israel and said to them, "Go and take for yourselves lambs according to your families, and slay the Passover lamb. You shall take a bunch of hyssop and dip it in the blood which is in the basin, and apply some of the blood that is in the basin to the lintel and the two doorposts; and none of you shall go outside the door of his house until morning. For the LORD will pass through to smite the Egyptians; and when He sees the blood on the lintel and on the two doorposts, the LORD will pass over the door and will not allow the destroyer to come in to your houses to smite you. (Exod. 12:21–23)*

The karpas, or parsley, is symbolic of the hyssop that the Israelites dipped into the blood and placed on their doors, demonstrating their faith and trust that God would fulfill the promise He had made concerning the slaying of the firstborn. Because of the blood, they were "passed over," and their firstborn sons were spared the tenth plague.

In hindsight we recognize that this is a picture of our deliverance from the consequences of sin, which includes not just physical death, but spiritual death or separation from God. Viewing the Seder in light of its fulfillment in Yeshua the Messiah, we see the dipping of the parsley in salt water as a declaration that one day all our tears will be wiped away (Rev. 21:4), and until then our sorrows are made sweet through knowing the Lord. When we put our faith in Him, His blood is placed over the doorposts and lintel of our hearts and lives. God sees that the blood of the Lamb covers our sin, His judgment passes over us, and we pass from death to life (John 5:24). The Lamb took our punishment upon Himself and we have been set free from the bondage of sin and death.

As the Apostle Paul writes to the Roman believers,

> But now having been freed from sin and enslaved to God, you derive your benefit, resulting in sanctification, and the outcome, eternal life. For the wages of sin is death, but the free gift of God is eternal life in Christ Jesus our Lord. (Rom. 6:22–23)

During Passover we look back at the biblical text through the lens of the modern Seder and see these beautiful parallels of redemption that help us explain the truths of the Gospel to our Jewish friends and even to our Gentile friends as well. We view the dipping of the parsley into salt water as a reminder of God's cure for the bitterness of life caused by sin. By linking the redemption found in Jesus to the Passover tradition, it will help your Jewish friends better understand what God has done for us through the Messiah.

SHARING THE GOOD NEWS THROUGH THE YACHATZ (BREAKING OF THE MIDDLE MATZAH)

The next Passover ceremony helping us share the Gospel with our Jewish friends is the *Yachatz* (literally, "divide"),

the breaking of the middle *matzah* (unleavened bread).
We set the Seder table with an item known as a *matzah
tash*—often a nicely embroidered pouch containing three
compartments, each holding a piece of matzah. Early in
the Seder, the leader picks up the matzah tash and explains
the significance of the three different pieces of matzah.
There are two traditional explanations. One view is that
the three compartments represent the Patriarchs: Abraham,
Isaac, and Jacob. A second interpretation is that they
represent the three categories of Jewish people: priests,
Levites, and laymen. Having identified the matzah tash,
the leader removes the middle piece of matzah, breaks it
in half, wraps one half in a linen cloth and hides it, so it
can be brought back at a later time in the ceremony.

Throughout the centuries, Jewish people have added
varying traditions to the Seder. But the source of this
tradition of the Yachatz, the breaking the middle matzah,
is unknown. Some Jewish scholars maintain that early
Jewish followers of Yeshua added it to their Seder and it
was adopted by traditional Judaism at a later date. There
are volumes of material written on the topic and in the
companion book, *Messiah in the Passover,* we have included
a chapter by Daniel Nessim that will enable you to further
explore this mysterious tradition.[8]

As Messianic Jews, we see the Passover ceremony through
three lenses: the Hebrew Scriptures, Jewish tradition, and
the New Testament, or New Covenant Scriptures. We are
not sure to what degree the Jewish traditions surrounding
the Yachatz had been developed during the time of Jesus.
Nonetheless, we can use this symbol to help explain the
Gospel to those we love.

---

8   See *The Gospel in the Passover's* companion book, *Messiah in the Passover,*
    chapter 11.

Based upon what is recorded in Luke 22, it seems possible that the ceremony involving the three pieces of matzah may have already been known by the time of the Last Supper. We do know that Yeshua identified with the broken matzah:

> *When He had taken some bread and given*
> *thanks, He broke it and gave it to them, saying,*
> *"This is My body which is given for you; do*
> *this in remembrance of Me'"*(Luke 22:19).

Therefore we find a good basis for explaining the Gospel in light of the Yachatz to our Jewish friends. It is wise to use known symbols and work our way forward, from the known to the unknown, in explaining the Gospel to those we love.

Most people raised in a Jewish home, celebrating the Passover every year, know what Yachatz is and understand the tradition of breaking the middle piece of matzah, wrapping it, hiding it, and bringing it back. This is why, when we present the Gospel through the Yachatz tradition, we are beginning with what is already well understood by our Jewish friends and linking this symbol to Jesus.

As Messianic Jews we see a third option for the symbolism of the matzah tash and its three compartments in that they represent the unity of God: Father, Son, and Holy Spirit, three in one, and one in three. We also see the breaking of the middle matzah as symbolic of our Messiah's death, the wrapping of the middle piece of matzah as speaking of His burial, and the bringing back of the hidden matzah as pointing to His resurrection. We are not dogmatically asserting that the modern Messianic view is exactly the same as the Passover ceremony celebrated by Jesus and His disciples. But we do know that during a Passover meal right before His arrest and crucifixion, Jesus broke a matzah and used it to represent His body, given for us (Luke 22:19). By using these traditional symbols you will be able to engage with your Jewish friends at a whole new level of familiarity. We pray this link between symbol and reality will help your friends better understand that the Gospel is not as foreign as most Jewish people are raised to believe.

SHARING THE GOOD NEWS THROUGH "DAYENU" ("IT WOULD HAVE BEEN ENOUGH")

During the Seder, the participants give thanks to God for all His benefits to us by singing a special song called "*Dayenu*" ("it would have been enough").[9] The song expresses the idea that if God had limited His gifts to Israel—it would have been enough and we would have been satisfied. Yet God, acting in His rich mercy, love, and faithfulness, did far more for us than we could ever imagine, and therefore we celebrate His great kindness.

Each verse of the song recounts an aspect of the Passover event, and after each verse we joyfully sing the chorus "*Dayenu*." For instance, one verse declares, "If He had merely rescued us from Egypt, but had not punished the Egyptians, it would have been enough." Other verses continue the celebration of all God did for us: He punished the Egyptians, destroyed their gods, slew their firstborn, gave us their property, split the Red Sea, gave us dry land on which to cross, drowned our enemies, sustained us in the desert for forty years, fed us manna, gave us the Torah, gave us the Shabbat, brought us to Mount Sinai, led us into the Promised Land, and built us a Temple. If He had not done any of these, it would have been enough and we would still have been satisfied.

---

9   For more on "*Dayenu,*" see the discussion by Scott Nassau, "The Celebration of Passover in Judaism and the Developing Church," in *The Gospel in the Passover's* companion book, *Messiah in the Passover,* chapter 7.

As followers of Yeshua, we can add one more verse that is not especially traditional! If God had only given us Messiah Yeshua and provided for our redemption through His death and resurrection, it would have been enough. Nevertheless, God gave us far more than the immediate gift of salvation. As Yeshua Himself said, *"I came that they may have life, and have it abundantly"* (John 10:10). It is true, and we are satisfied that through believing the good news, the message about the death and resurrection of the Messiah Yeshua, we have been granted forgiveness of sin and the gift of eternal life. Yet, He gives us so much more. He generously provides us with an abundant life filled with love, joy, peace, fulfillment, and purpose.

The *"Dayenu"* song reminds us that by believing the good news of Yeshua we will be satisfied for all eternity. The moment of salvation is just the beginning of the abundant life we will enjoy forever. This is why one of the best ways to communicate the Gospel to your Jewish friends is to share your personal testimony. Do not stop at the point where you embraced Yeshua as your Lord and Savior— continue on to tell your friends about the great blessings, answers to prayer, and joy you have received because you know and serve Him. Your testimony is the most powerful tool you have to demonstrate the truth of the Gospel. You can also encourage your friends to go online and watch the video testimonies posted on the **I Found Shalom** site (ifoundshalom.com). It will be a great blessing to them and will help them understand why you are shouting *Dayenu*!

SHARING THE GOOD NEWS THROUGH THE *ZEROAH* (SHANKBONE)

Rabban Gamaliel, who appears in the Book of Acts, said that in order for one to discharge his Passover duty, he must discuss three elements: the shankbone of a lamb, the matzah, and the bitter herb.[10] Therefore, after the "*Dayenu*" song, the Seder leader picks up a lamb shankbone to discuss this essential part of the Seder. The Seder plate includes a place for the *zeroah*, or shankbone of a lamb, in order to recall the sacrificial lambs of the first Passover. Regarding that Egyptian Passover, God commands Moses,

> *Speak to all the congregation of Israel, saying, "On the tenth of this month they are each one to take a lamb for themselves, according to their fathers' households, a lamb for each household. . . . Your lamb shall be an unblemished male a year old; you may take it from the sheep or from the goats. . . . You shall keep it until the fourteenth day of the same month, then the whole assembly of the congregation of Israel is to kill it at twilight. . . . They shall eat the flesh that same night, roasted with fire, and they shall eat it with unleavened bread and bitter herbs." (Exod. 12:3, 5, 6, 8)*

A change does occur later in the unfolding of the Torah. Moses tells the people of Israel,

> *You are not allowed to sacrifice the Passover in any of your towns which the LORD your God is giving*

---

10 See Mishnah *Pesahim* 10:5. Some have conjectured that the reason for Gamaliel's inclusion of these three Passover essentials is as a response to early followers of Yeshua. From an early date, followers of Yeshua identified the lamb with Yeshua, the Lamb of God who takes away the sin of the world; the matzah with the body of Yeshua, given as a sacrificial atonement as expressed in the Eucharist (Lord's Supper or Communion); and the bitter herbs, descriptive of the suffering of Yeshua for sin. Hence, Gamaliel called for a discussion of these elements to counter those interpretations, since they so clearly depict Yeshua. Professor of Jewish History Israel J. Yuval states, "Rabban Gamaliel is demanding a declaration of loyalty to the Jewish interpretations and, therefore, an implicit denial of the Christian alternative" ("Easter and Passover as Early Jewish-Christian Dialogue," in *Passover and Easter: Origin and History to Modern Times*, ed. Paul F. Bradshaw and Lawrence A. Hoffman, Two Liturgical Traditions 5 (Notre Dame, IN: Notre Dame Press: 1999), 107.

you; but at the place where the LORD your God
chooses to establish His name, you shall sacrifice
the Passover in the evening at sunset, at the time
that you came out of Egypt. (Deut. 16:5–6)

So, in time, the sacrifice of the lambs became attached to the Temple.

However, after the Temple was destroyed in 70 A.D., there was no longer a place to perform this sacrifice, and eating lamb as part of the Seder became a point of disagreement within the wider Jewish community. As the years went by, the raising of the shankbone of a lamb became a symbol of the destruction of the Temple and the sacrifices of previous days. Presently, due to differences in rabbinic rulings Sephardic Jews eat lamb as part of their Passover tradition, but for Ashkenazic Jews lamb too closely resembles the pascal lamb sacrifice, so they eat chicken, beef or turkey instead.

In the book of Leviticus, God gives the Jewish people instructions through Moses regarding the full range of sacrifices. There are many different types of offerings, including those sacrificed on behalf of the Israelites as atonement for their sin. The offerings of the Passover are not specifically identified in that way, but when viewed through the lens of the original Passover sacrifice and linked to the Last Supper of Jesus, it is easy to see the Passover sacrifice as another substitutionary offering that serves as a type of the ultimate sacrifice God will effect through the work of His Son. This gives new and deeper meaning to the heart cry of John the Baptist:

The next day he saw Jesus coming to him and
said, "Behold, the Lamb of God who takes
away the sin of the world!" (John 1:29)

The New Covenant Scriptures declare that the offerings of sheep and goats could never take away sin, but they were prophetic shadows and types of the once-for-all offering of our Messiah Yeshua (Heb. 10:4). And the Prophet Isaiah speaks of the Servant of the Lord who will function as the true Lamb that is to come for all Israel and the world.

> *But He was pierced through for our transgressions,*
>   *He was crushed for our iniquities;*
> *the chastening for our well-being fell upon Him,*
>   *and by His scourging we are healed.*
>
> *All of us like sheep have gone astray,*
>   *each of us has turned to his own way;*
> *but the* LORD *has caused the iniquity*
> *of us all to fall on Him.*
>
> *He was oppressed and He was afflicted,*
>   *yet He did not open His mouth;*
>   *like a lamb that is led to slaughter,*
> *and like a sheep that is silent before its shearers,*
>   *so He did not open His mouth.* (Isa. 53:5–7)

Although the shankbone is a "stand-in" for the lamb no longer offered, we also recognize that the Passover sacrifice was itself a type or "stand-in" for the future Messiah who would take away the sin of the world. When the Israelites in Egypt placed the blood of their sacrificial Passover lambs on the doorposts of their houses, God "passed over" them and judged Egypt by slaying their firstborn males.

In the same way, when anyone today applies the blood of Messiah Yeshua to the doorposts of their heart by faith, God promises that His holy judgment will "pass over." All who put their trust in Messiah's death as their Passover Lamb will experience the promise of salvation and deliverance from the bondage of sin and death. The Gospel can clearly be seen in lifting up the shankbone of the lamb during the Seder meal.

It is our hope and prayer that your Jewish friend will see this connection between the Exodus story, the Passover Seder, and Yeshua. May God give you wisdom in explaining these profound truths to your Jewish friends.

SHARING THE GOOD NEWS THROUGH THE *MATZAH*

Rabban Gamaliel's second Passover essential, after the lamb shankbone, is to include a discussion of the *matzah* (unleavened bread). The leader of the Seder raises a piece of the matzah and tells the story of how the people of Israel were forced to flee Egypt in great haste. They had no time to bake their bread and could not wait for the dough to rise. The sun then beat down on the dough as they carried it along and baked it into unleavened bread called matzah. According to the Torah,

> *"They baked the dough which they had brought out of Egypt into cakes of unleavened bread. For it had not become leavened, since they were driven out of Egypt and could not delay, nor had they prepared any provisions for themselves."* (Exod. 12:39)

Messianic believers in Yeshua include reflections on intriguing parallels between matzah and the Messiah. After all, He is not only the Lamb of God, but also the bread of life. Matzah is unleavened, is made striped, and has holes or pierce marks. Each of these illustrates truths about Yeshua the Messiah.

Leaven in Scripture is frequently a symbol of sin (cf. 1 Cor. 5:6–8; Matt. 16:6). Therefore, the bread without leaven reminds us of Messiah's purity as He lived life on earth without sin (Heb. 4:15). This was predicted by the prophet Isaiah, when speaking of Messiah's brutal death, indicating that *"He had done no violence, nor was there any deceit in His mouth"* (Isa. 53:9; cf. 1 Peter 2:22).

The matzah is striped as Yeshua was striped by a Roman whip. This reminds us of Isaiah's prediction that *"by His scourging we are healed"* (Isa. 53:5).

Additionally, the matzah is pierced.[11] It was foretold that the Servant of the Lord would be pierced for our sins. The prophet Isaiah wrote:

> *Surely our griefs He Himself bore,*
>   *and our sorrows He carried;*
> *yet we ourselves esteemed Him stricken,*
>   *smitten of God, and afflicted.*
>
> *But He was pierced through for our transgressions,*
>   *He was crushed for our iniquities;*
> *the chastening for our well-being fell*
>   *upon Him.* (Isa. 53:4–5)

This is also what David predicted one thousand years before Yeshua's crucifixion,

> *For dogs have surrounded me;*
>   *a band of evildoers has encompassed me;*
> *they pierced my hands and my feet.*
>   *I can count all my bones.*
> *They look, they stare at me;*
>   *they divide my garments among them,*
>   *and for my clothing they cast lots.* (Ps. 22:16–18)

---

11 Perforating matzah has always been the tradition in order to slow down the fermentation process (cf. Ari Greenspan, Ari Z. Zivotofsky, and Elli Wohlgelernter. "Matzah." In *Encyclopedia Judaica*, edited by Fred Skolnik and Michael Berenbaum, 13:689–70. 2nd ed. 22 vols. Detroit: Macmillan Reference USA, 2007).

The great prophet Zechariah foretold the day when the Jewish people would recognize Yeshua as Israel's Messiah.

> *I will pour out on the house of David and on the inhabitants of Jerusalem, the Spirit of grace and of supplication, so that they will look on Me whom they have pierced; and they will mourn for Him, as one mourns for an only son, and they will weep bitterly over Him like the bitter weeping over a firstborn.* (Zech. 12:10)

The matzah is essential both to the story of the Exodus and to the life and witness of Yeshua and His suffering. It reveals a crucial element of the good news: a sinless Messiah will be striped with a Roman whip and pierced by a Roman spear and cruel nails, all to redeem us from slavery to sin.

Sharing the Good News through the *Beitzah* (Egg)

Another element on the Passover Seder plate is the *beitzah* (egg), which is both hardboiled and roasted. Although the egg is a traditional element on the Seder plate, it is notable that nothing in the Passover liturgy discusses it. Traditionally, the egg is peeled and dipped in salt water before it is eaten.

It reminds us of a second type of offering, the Festival Offering, the *hagigah* in Hebrew, which was brought to the Temple on each of the *Shalosh Regalim* (lit., "three feet," meaning the three pilgrimage holidays): Passover (*Pesach*), Pentecost (*Shavuot*), and Tabernacles (*Sukkot*).

> *Three times in a year all your males shall appear before the LORD your God in the place which He chooses, at the Feast of Unleavened Bread and at the Feast of Weeks and at the Feast of Booths, and they shall not appear*

*before the LORD empty-handed. Every man shall give
as he is able, according to the blessing of the LORD your
God which He has given you.* (Deut. 16:16–17)

Traditionally, this represented an additional festival
sacrifice. Since the Holy Temple was destroyed in 70 A.D.
by the Romans, it is no longer possible to offer the
sacrifice. Therefore, the egg is used to commemorate this
annual *hagigah* sacrifice. We show our sorrow over the
Temple's destruction by dipping the egg in salt water
(symbolic of tears) and eating it.

Followers of Messiah Yeshua have good news—Messiah
came and offered Himself as a final sacrifice, making
salvation available for all who trust in Him. The writer of
Hebrews says that *"not through the blood of goats and calves,
but through His own blood, He [Messiah Yeshua] entered the
holy place* once for all, *having obtained eternal redemption"*
(Heb. 9:12, emphasis added). He goes on to say that
Messiah was *"offered once to bear the sins of many"* (v. 28).

There is no need to lament the lack of availability of the
festival sacrifice. So, why would a Messianic believer still eat
the egg in salt water? The answer is to express sorrow for all
those who do not yet know and believe in the good news
of Messiah Yeshua's ultimate and eternal sacrifice.

SHARING THE GOOD NEWS THROUGH THE *AFIKOMAN* (BROKEN MATZAH)

After the actual Passover meal and just prior to partaking
of the third cup (the cup of redemption), it is traditional
to search for the matzah that was broken and hidden
earlier in the Seder (see discussion above on the *Yachatz*).
Remember, the middle piece of matzah was removed
from the matzah tash, broken, wrapped in a linen cloth,

and then hidden. After the meal, the children search for this hidden matzah. Once it is found, the leader purchases it back from the finder and distributes olive-size pieces of the matzah for all participants to eat.

The origin of this tradition and of its name, the *afikoman*, is unclear.[12] Traditionally, Judaism defines the word *afikoman* as "dessert," and thus it is the last food to be eaten after the meal. Even the cakes and other Passover desserts must be consumed before the afikoman. While the Temple still stood, participants in a Seder would save a piece of the sacrificial Passover lamb as the final food consumed. Thus, the last taste on a person's palate would be the lamb, so central to the celebration and commemoration of Passover.[13]

One explanation for the afikoman is that it harks back to a custom begun by early Jewish followers of the Messiah Yeshua, which involved eating a small piece of matzah instead of lamb at the close of the Passover meal. Some Jewish scholars suggest that after the destruction of the Temple, traditional Judaism adopted this substitution of matzah for lamb without recognizing its symbolic significance for early Jewish followers of Yeshua.[14] As for the word *afikoman* itself, although traditionally defined as "dessert," its derivation is from Greek and actually means "the one who has come," a clear Messianic title.[15]

---

12 For more on the afikoman tradition, see Daniel Nessim, "Passover and the Afikoman," in companion book, *Messiah in the Passover,* chapter 11.

13 See Mishnah *Pesahim* 10:8 and Babylonian Talmud *Pesahim* 119b–120a.

14 This was first proposed in a two-part article appearing in a German language journal by Austrian Jewish scholar Robert Eisler, "Das Letzte Abendmahl" (Part 1), *Zeitschrift für die neutestamentliche Wissenschaft und die Kunde der älteren Kirche* 24 (1925): 161–92; Robert Eisler, "Das Letzte Abendmahl" (Part 2), *Zeitschrift für die neutestamentliche Wissenschaft und die Kunde der älteren Kirche* 25 (1926): 5–37.

15 The twentieth century's preeminent Jewish scholar of ancient and biblical law, David Daube, supports Eisler's view that the afikoman came from the Seders of ancient Jewish followers of Yeshua and is derived

With this in mind, the significance of eating the afikoman becomes apparent. As all participants prepare to partake of the third cup, the middle matzah that was previously broken, wrapped in linen, and hidden is now returned to complete the memorial meal. This piece of matzah now represents the body of Yeshua, offered as a sacrifice.

Two thousand years ago, Yeshua took the matzah and told His followers, *"Take, eat; this is my body," "which is given for you"* (Matt. 26:26; Luke 22:19; cf. 1 Cor. 11:24). Just like the Passover lamb pointed to the Messiah, so the bread points back to our Messiah Yeshua. The breaking of the middle matzah is a picture of the death of the Messiah. When we add the search for the afikoman and its return, or Yeshua's resurrection, to the Seder table, there is a powerful picture of the Gospel, namely, the death and resurrection of Messiah Yeshua.

While especially meaningful to believers in Yeshua, these symbols also enable you to share the story of the Gospel with nonbelievers in a very picturesque way. This is a wonderful tool to tell your Jewish friends the very Jewish story of Passover's ultimate fulfillment in Yeshua.

SHARING THE GOOD NEWS THROUGH THE THIRD CUP (THE CUP OF REDEMPTION)

After the eating of the afikoman, the Seder participants turn their attention to the third cup, called the Cup of

from the Greek Messianic title, meaning "the one who has come" (cf. David Daube, *He That Cometh* (London: Diocesan Council, 1966), 6–14; reprinted in David Daube, *New Testament Judaism*, vol. 2 of *Collected Works of David Daube*, ed. Calum M. Carmichael, Studies in Comparative Legal History (Berkeley: Robbins Collection Publications / University of California at Berkeley, 2000), 429–40). His views on the origins of the Eucharist and its connection to the Seder are also discussed in his article, "The Earliest Structure of the Gospels," *New Testament Studies* 5, no. 3 (1959), 174–87.

Redemption. This cup represents the price of redemption for the deliverance of the people of Israel from Egyptian bondage. Through Moses, God told the Israelites to sacrifice a lamb and smear its blood upon the doorposts and lintels of their houses. On that first Passover, at midnight, when the Lord passed through Egypt, He struck down the firstborn in the land. All the people who placed the blood on their houses were spared the death of their firstborn, as God had promised:

> For I will go through the land of Egypt on that night, and will strike down all the firstborn in the land of Egypt, both man and beast; and against all the gods of Egypt I will execute judgments—I am the LORD. The blood shall be a sign for you on the houses where you live; and when I see the blood I will pass over you, and no plague will befall you to destroy you when I strike the land of Egypt. (Exod. 12:12–13)

The cup of redemption symbolizes the purchase price paid for the release of the people of Israel from Egypt. It also speaks of a greater purchase price, for our redemption from sin and death through the shed blood of Yeshua.

Yeshua took the cup after the meal and said, *"This cup which is poured out for you is the new covenant in my blood"* (Luke 22:20). The blood of the Passover lamb pointed to this greater story of redemption: that Yeshua would die, pour out His blood, and redeem all those who would believe by faith and put their trust in Him. The Apostle Peter writes,

> You were not redeemed with perishable things like silver or gold from your futile way of life inherited from your forefathers, but with precious blood, as of a lamb unblemished and spotless, the blood of Christ. (1 Peter 1:18–19)

The good news of the Gospel flows from the cup each time our lips touch the sweet fruit of the vine proclaiming the magnificent truth of Yeshua's sacrificial death for all. As Paul again writes to the mostly Gentile Corinthian believers,

> *In the same way He took the cup also after supper, saying, "This cup is the new covenant in My blood; do this, as often as you drink it, in remembrance of Me." For as often as you eat this bread and drink the cup, you proclaim the Lord's death until He comes.* (1 Cor. 11:25–26)

Remember, your Jewish friends are not familiar with the Christian tradition of the Lord's Supper or Communion. However, with some patient explanation, you can help them understand how important the Passover is to you and that it is the very basis for your salvation. They will be astonished to learn that a Jewish tradition fulfilled by Jesus means so much to you personally. This is a great way to build common ground between yourself and the Jewish people you are praying will become followers of the Lamb of God.

SHARING THE GOOD NEWS THROUGH ELIYAHU (THE CUP OF ELIJAH)

Near the conclusion of the Passover Seder, there is a significant ceremony related to the prophet Elijah. In fact, Elijah is the invited guest to every Seder. Therefore, there is always an extra place setting for Elijah at each Seder. If 20 people will be attending the Seder, the table must be set for 21. If 100 attend, there must be 101 place settings.

According to the prophet Malachi, God's messenger must come before the Messiah to usher in the times of the Lord. He writes,

> *"Behold, I am going to send My messenger, and he
> will clear the way before Me. And the Lord, whom
> you seek, will suddenly come to His temple; and the
> messenger of the covenant, in whom you delight, behold,
> He is coming," says the* LORD *of hosts.* (Mal. 3:1)

Furthermore, the prophet declares,

> *Behold, I am going to send you Elijah the
> prophet before the coming of the great and
> terrible day of the* LORD. (Mal. 4:5)

According to Jewish tradition, Elijah will announce the
coming of the Messiah during the Passover Seder. So at
the end of the meal, the leader will have someone go to
the door to see if Elijah is there. When the door is opened,
the leader will ask if Elijah has come tonight. When told
that he has not, the leader states that Elijah is not here
tonight and that maybe next year he will come, in which
case we would all celebrate Passover in Jerusalem with the
Messiah for whom we wait.

According to the New Covenant Scriptures, someone did
come who was like Elijah. He wore a similar garment,
belt, ate a similar diet, and preached a message of
repentance in the desert. His message was to turn back to
God and prepare for the coming of the Messiah.

When the disciples asked Yeshua why Elijah must come
first, He replied that Elijah is still coming and will restore all
things. But Yeshua added that in a sense, Elijah already came
(Matt. 17:12). To explain what He meant, He declared that
if they cared to accept it, John the Baptist is the Elijah who
was to come. Certainly, he was not stating that John was
literally Elijah, but that John had come in the power and
spirit of Elijah. Jesus goes on to say that they (the Jewish
leaders) did not recognize John, but did to him whatever

they wished. Yeshua compared this rejection of John to the Jewish leaders' rejection of Him; Yeshua had come, but Israel's leaders did not recognize Him as their Messiah and would do to Him as they wished also.

How sad that during Passover, Jewish people all over the world say that Elijah is not here and do not realize that he did indeed come. We missed John the Baptizer who had come in the power and spirit of Elijah, and also missed that Yeshua, the Messiah had come soon thereafter.

It is during the cup of Elijah that Messianic Jewish celebrants declare that Elijah has already come and introduced the Messiah, Yeshua, to the world. It is John who said, *"'I am not the Christ,' but 'I have been sent before Him'"* (John 3:28).

At the conclusion of the Seder, the long wait begins again. The cup of Elijah is poured into the sink and the Jewish people sing the poignant song, "Next Year in Jerusalem." How heartbreaking it is to realize that John indeed was an Elijah-like prophet who had prepared the way for the Lord. And the Lord Himself had come—Jesus the Messiah— though not exactly as expected. He came in humility to fulfill the mandate of His first coming—to suffer and die for the sins of both Jews and Gentiles. His second coming will be quite different. At that point, He will come to judge the living and the dead and to establish His kingdom in Jerusalem as promised. We look forward to that great day and with the Jewish community sing, "Next Year in Jerusalem," hoping that He will return soon.

Until then, we rejoice in the holy obligation given to us to share the good news with our Jewish friends and neighbors, proclaiming that the Messiah has come.

CONCLUSION

In so many ways, the Passover Seder makes the Good News Jewish-friendly and profoundly clear. If people are open to God and His message, the elements of the Seder will speak to their hearts and reveal the truth that Yeshua is the Messiah of Israel, the Passover Lamb (Rom. 10:1; 1 Cor. 5:7).

Yeshua's death, burial, and resurrection are observed from the very beginning of the dipping of the parsley to the last cup at the table, the cup of Elijah. It is these elements that make it possible to use the Passover Seder to explain the Gospel to your Jewish friends and relatives.

He is the One who came, the Bread of Life, the Lamb of God, and He provides the cup of salvation to all who drink. This is the glorious message He has given us to share with our friends; to the Jew first and also to the Gentiles. May the Lord empower and bless you as you show how the Passover points to Jesus the Messiah.

5

A MESSIANIC FAMILY HAGGADAH

CHOSEN PEOPLE MINISTRIES

The following Messianic Family Haggadah is designed for use with your family, home group, or church to celebrate a Jesus-centered Passover Seder. You are permitted to make copies of the Haggadah from this book for this purpose or go to www.messiahinthepassover.com and download a printable copy for those attending your Seder. Additional Passover-themed resources such as song suggestions for the Seder are also available on this website.

♥♥♥

For many centuries, Passover has been celebrated with the help of a Haggadah, a book or booklet that includes liturgy, stories, participatory reading, and biblical references to guide Jewish families in their celebration of this holy festival. The Haggadah, which means "the telling," was compiled by Jewish sages over hundreds and perhaps thousands of years. You will find many versions of the Haggadah from Jewish cultures around the world that tell the story of God's redemption of the people of Israel from bondage in Egypt.

This particular Haggadah, based upon the traditional order of service of the Passover, is adapted for use by both Jewish and Gentile followers of Yeshua (Jesus). Along with the usual elements of the Seder, we highlight the links between the traditional Seder and the Last Supper. It is our prayer that you will set aside time during Passover week and enjoy a Seder together with family and friends, so that your faith in the Lamb of God who takes away the sin of the world will be deepened, or even perhaps awakened for the first time if you have not yet committed your life to God's Messiah.

The word *Seder* simply means "order" and refers to an order of service designed to tell the story of the Passover. This telling (Haggadah) reminds the children of Israel each year of what God did by the hand of Moses in delivering them from Egyptian bondage. This is a great way to enhance your understanding of Scripture. The Feast of Passover is especially for the children, as they can personally participate in the Seder. By touching, tasting, and smelling the elements on the Seder table, participants are brought back to the great events of the original Exodus and become better able to identify with the Exodus and the redemption of the children of Israel.

Yet, for followers of the Messiah, the story of redemption reminds us of far more than the deliverance from Egypt. It brings our minds to the redemption and deliverance from sin that God has provided through His Son. We believe that Yeshua celebrated an early form of the Passover Seder with His disciples. This Haggadah, especially created for you and your family, will wed these two great stories of redemption together, as we join the Savior on that night when He celebrated His last Seder with His disciples on this earth.

Order of Service (Seder)

Birkat HaNer, Lighting of the Candles

Kiddush, First Cup: The Cup of Sanctification

Urchatz, First Washing of the Hands

Karpas, Dipping of the Parsley

Yachatz, Breaking of the Middle Matzah

Maggid, The Story of the Passover

Ma-Nishtanah, The Four Questions

Makkot, Second Cup: The Cup of Plagues

Zeroah, or *Pesach*, The Lamb Shankbone

Rachtzah, Second Washing of the Hands

Maror, Eating of the Bitter Herbs

Korech, Eating of the Bitter Herbs with Charoset

Beitzah, The Roasted Egg

Shulchan Orech, The Passover Supper

Tzafun, Eating of the Afikoman

HaGeulah, Third Cup: The Cup of Redemption

Eliyahu, Elijah's Cup

Hallel, Fourth Cup: The Cup of Praise

Birkat HaNer, Lighting of the Candles

Traditionally, Passover is celebrated at home with family after all leaven has been removed from the household. Once the house and the participants are ceremonially clean, the Passover Seder can begin. The woman of the house says a blessing and lights the Passover candles. It is appropriate that the woman brings light into the home, because it was through the woman that the light of the world, Messiah Jesus, came into the world (Gen. 3:15; Luke 2:7).

The woman of the house recites the following Hebrew prayer:

בָּרוּךְ אַתָּה אֲדֹנָי אֱלֹהֵינוּ מֶלֶךְ הָעוֹלָם אֲשֶׁר
קִדְּשָׁנוּ בְּמִצְוֹתָיו וְצִוָּנוּ לְהַדְלִיק נֵר שֶׁל יוֹם טוֹב.

*Baruch atah Ado-nai Elo-hei-nu Melech
ha-Olam, asher kid-sha-nu bemits-vo-tav
vetsi-va-nu lehad-lik ner shel yom tov.*

Blessed art Thou, O Lord our God, King
of the universe, who has sanctified us with
Thy commandments and commanded
us to kindle the festival lights.

THE FOUR CUPS OF THE FRUIT OF THE VINE

The Passover Seder is structured around four cups of the fruit of the vine, which serve as the foundation for the experience. Each cup is named after one of the four specific promises that God made to Israel in Exodus 6:6–7. Each cup is thematically connected to a different stage in the progression of the Seder.

1. The Cup of Sanctification
2. The Cup of Plagues
3. The Cup of Redemption
4. The Cup of Praise

KIDDUSH, FIRST CUP: THE CUP OF SANCTIFICATION

The Seder begins with a blessing recited over the first cup, the Cup of Sanctification (also called the Cup of Blessing). This first cup is meant to sanctify—to set apart—the rest of the evening as a holy occasion. We fill the cup until it overflows, as in Jewish tradition a full cup is a symbol of joy. Passover moves us to rejoice and celebrate God's goodness to His people. As a symbol of freedom, we drink comfortably leaning to the left.

All fill the cup. The leader recites the blessing and all drink leaning to the left:

בָּרוּךְ אַתָּה אֲדֹנָי אֱלֹהֵינוּ מֶלֶךְ הָעוֹלָם בּוֹרֵא פְּרִי הַגָּפֶן.

Baruch atah Ado-nai Elo-hei-nu Melech ha-Olam, bo-ray pri ha-gah-fen.

Blessed art Thou, O Lord our God, King of the universe, Creator of the fruit of the vine.

URCHATZ, WASHING OF THE HANDS (JOHN 13:1–11)

This first washing of the hands is a symbolic gesture of personal sanctification as we enter into the holy celebration of the Passover. Traditionally, two children carry a pitcher, a basin, and a towel and go around the table pouring a little water on the guests' hands, starting with the leader of the Seder.

KARPAS, DIPPING OF THE PARSLEY (EXODUS 12:21–22)

The parsley symbolizes the hyssop used to place the blood of the Passover lamb upon the doorposts and lintels of the homes of the children of Israel during the tenth and most terrible plague that the Lord visited upon Egypt—the slaying of the firstborn. The salt water represents the tears of the children of Israel and the Red Sea. We are therefore reminded of the tears shed by those not yet redeemed and still in slavery. This is a good time to mention those around the world who are hurting and enslaved.

All dip a sprig of parsley in the salted water, the leader
recites the blessing, all eat the parsley.

בָּרוּךְ אַתָּה אֲדֹנָי אֱלֹהֵינוּ מֶלֶךְ הָעוֹלָם בּוֹרֵא פְּרִי הָאֲדָמָה.

*Ba-ruch Atah Adonai Elo-hei-nu Me-lech
ha-Olam, boh-ray pri ha-adamah.*

Blessed art Thou, O Lord our God, King of the
universe, Creator of the fruit of the earth.

———

YACHATZ, BREAKING OF THE MIDDLE MATZAH

One of the central elements of the Passover is *matzah*
(unleavened bread). For the Passover Seder, three separate
sheets of matzah are inserted into a bag with three compartments, known as the *matzah tash*.

In Jewish tradition, this three-in-one bag has many in-
terpretations. It is said to represent the three Patriarchs:
Abraham, Isaac, and Jacob; or the three kinds of people of
Israel: the priests, the Levites, and the masses. Believers in
Yeshua suggest that this could be a representation of the tri-
une nature of God: the Father, the Son, and the Holy Spirit.

The leader takes the middle matzah, breaks it in two and
puts one half back in the middle of the matzah tash. He
then wraps the other half, now known as the afikoman,
in a white napkin and hides it. This hidden matzah will
reappear at the conclusion of the Passover meal.

———

MAGGID, THE STORY OF THE PASSOVER
(READ EXODUS 12:1–15)

It is tradition to read the story of the Passover every year
at the Seder, to ensure that every generation keeps the
memory of Israel's deliverance from slavery alive.

MA-NISHTANAH, THE FOUR QUESTIONS

As the retelling of the Exodus story begins, the youngest child (who can read!) asks the Four Questions to the leader of the Seder. You might choose to have all the children read together, have one child ask each question, or ask one child to read them all.

מַה נִּשְׁתַּנָה הַלַּיְלָה הַזֶּה מִכָּל הַלֵּילוֹת?

Mah nish-ta-nah ha-lai-lah ha-zeh mi-kohl ha-lay-lot?

In English:

"Why is this night so different from all other nights?"

1. "On all other nights we eat bread with leaven. On this night why do we eat only matzah?"

2. "On all other nights we eat all kinds of vegetables; on this night why do we eat only bitter herbs?"

3. "On all other nights we never think of dipping herbs in water or in anything else; why on this night do we dip the parsley in salt water?"

4. "On all other nights we eat either sitting or reclining; on this night why do we eat only reclining?"

The leader of the Seder responds to the questions with the traditional answer:

We were slaves to Pharaoh in Egypt, and God brought us out with a strong hand and an outstretched arm. And if God had not brought our ancestors out of Egypt, we and our children and our children's children would still be subjugated to Pharaoh in Egypt. Even if we were all old and wise and learned in Torah, we would still be commanded to tell the story of the Exodus from Egypt.

The Ten Plagues

Each Passover cup is a symbolic full cup of joy except for the second cup—the Cup of Plagues—because God teaches us never to rejoice over the fate of our enemies. For this reason, the filling of the second cup must be reduced.

The second cup is filled. The leader of the Seder leads the group in a recitation of the ten plagues that the Lord poured out upon the Egyptians.

To reduce the second cup, each participant dips their little finger into the cup, removing one drop and placing it onto a plate in front of them, once for each plague. The names of the plagues are recited in unison as the drops are removed.

> Blood! Frogs! Gnats! Flies! Pestilence! Boils! Hail! Locusts! Darkness! Slaying of the Firstborn!

"Dayenu," It Would Have Been Enough

Just as we do not rejoice over the fate of our enemies, we also recognize the magnitude of God's salvation and His gracious actions toward us. With a grateful heart and a healthy fear of the Lord, we sing *"Dayenu"* ("it would have satisfied us") together, remembering the many great acts that God has done on behalf of His people.

> *Ilu hotzi, hotzianu, hotzianu miMitzrayim, hotzianu miMitzrayim, dayenu!*
>
> *Dai-dai-yenu, dai-dai-yenu, dai-dai-yenu, dayenu, dayenu!*
>
> *Had God done nothing but save us from the land of Egypt, for that alone we would have been satisfied!*

Ilu natan natan lanu, natan lanu et haTorah,
natan lanu et haTorah, dayenu!

Dai-dai-yenu, dai-dai-yenu, dai-dai-yenu, dayenu, dayenu!

Had God given us nothing more than the Torah,
for that alone we would have been satisfied!

Ilu natan natan lanu, natan lanu et Yeshua,
natan lanu et Yeshua, dayenu!

Dai-dai-yenu, dai-dai-yenu, dai-dai-yenu, dayenu, dayenu!

Had God given us nothing more than Yeshua,
for that alone we would have been satisfied (yet
He continues to give us so much more)!

MAKKOT, SECOND CUP: THE CUP OF PLAGUES

The reduced second cup, the Cup of Plagues (also called the Cup of Judgment), is raised and all recite the following:

Truly, we can say Hallelujah for the great redemption that God has wrought on our behalf, redemption at a terrible price: in Egypt, the death of the first born; for us, redemption from sin, the death of God's Son. *"For God so loved the world, that He gave His only begotten Son, that whoever believes in Him shall not perish, but have eternal life."* (John 3:16)

This is also a good time to sing a chorus or two about God's love and Yeshua's sacrifice for our sins.

The leader recites the blessing, all drink leaning to the left:

בָּרוּךְ אַתָּה אֲדֹנָי אֱלֹהֵינוּ מֶלֶךְ הָעוֹלָם בּוֹרֵא פְּרִי הַגָּפֶן.

Baruch Atah Adonai Elo-hei-nu Me-lech
ha-Olam, boh-ray pri ha-gah-fen.

Blessed art Thou, O Lord our God, King of the universe, Creator of the fruit of the vine.

ZEROAH OR *PESACH*, THE LAMB SHANKBONE

The lamb shankbone is a symbol of the Temple sacrifice. It sits on the Passover plate as a reminder of the first Passover lamb sacrificed for the children of Israel, whose blood was applied to the lintel and doorposts of their homes. We raise the shankbone of the lamb and again remind ourselves of the lamb slain on behalf of the firstborn males among the Jewish people. We also take this moment to reflect upon the death of Jesus for our sins, as He was the Lamb of God who takes away the sin of the world (John 1:29). We explain to our children the nature of redemption and the need for the shedding of blood for all of us to experience forgiveness of sin (Lev. 17:11; Heb. 9:22).

It might be appropriate to read all or part of Isaiah 52:13–53:12 at this time as a way to remember the work of Jesus the Messiah on our behalf.

RACHTZAH, SECOND WASHING OF THE HANDS

The second symbolic washing of the hands reinforces personal sanctification as we continue the celebration of the Passover. Yeshua appears to have taken Rachtzah one step further by washing the feet of His disciples, providing us with an unparalleled lesson in servanthood and humility (John 13:2–17). This second washing is followed by a blessing:

בָּרוּךְ אַתָּה אֲדֹנָי אֱלֹהֵינוּ מֶלֶךְ הָעוֹלָם אֲשֶׁר קִדְּשָׁנוּ בְּמִצְוֹתָיו
וְצִוָּנוּ עַל נְטִלַת יָדָיִם.

Ba-ruch Atah Adonai Elo-hei-nu Me-lech ha-Olam, ash-er kid-sha-nu b'mits-vo-tav v'tsi-va-nu al ne-tee-lat ya-dayim.

124

Blessed art Thou, O Lord our God, King of the universe, who sanctified us with His commandments, and commanded us concerning the washing of hands.

MOTZI, MATZOT

As the first portion of the Seder draws to a close, the family partakes of several of the remaining elements on the Seder plate. These elements are intended to involve our senses in the remembrance of the Passover story. Each one helps us connect with a different step in the process of Israel's deliverance from slavery. For believers in Yeshua, these elements remind us of the process of deliverance from our slavery to sin to our freedom in Messiah.

The matzah tash is raised and the following blessing is recited.

בָּרוּךְ אַתָּה אֲדֹנָי אֱלֹהֵינוּ מֶלֶךְ הָעוֹלָם הַמּוֹצִיא לֶחֶם מִן הָאָרֶץ.

Ba-ruch Atah Adonai Elo-hei-nu Me-lech ha-Olam, Ha-mo-tzi le-chem min hah-ah-retz.

Blessed art Thou, O Lord our God, King of the universe, who brings forth bread from the earth.

Each person now breaks off a small piece of matzah and all recite the following blessing:

בָּרוּךְ אַתָּה אֲדֹנָי אֱלֹהֵינוּ מֶלֶךְ הָעוֹלָם אֲשֶׁר קִדְּשָׁנוּ בְּמִצְוֹתָיו
וְצִוָּנוּ עַל אֲכִלַת מַצָּה.

Ba-ruch Atah Adonai Elo-hei-nu Me-lech ha-Olam, ash-er kid-sha-nu b'mits-vo-tav v'tsi-va-nu al a-chi-lat ma-tzah.

Blessed art Thou, O Lord our God, King of the universe, who sanctified us with His commandments, and commanded us concerning the eating of unleavened bread.

All eat together of the matzah.

―――

MAROR, EATING OF THE BITTER HERBS

The *maror* (bitter herbs) reminds us of the bitterness of
Israel's slavery in Egypt and the bitterness of humankind's
slavery to sin. It is tradition to dip one's matzah and take
a heaping portion of the bitter herb, enough to make one
shed a tear.

Each person breaks an olive-sized piece of matzah and
dips it in the bitter herbs. The following blessing is recited:

בָּרוּךְ אַתָּה אֲדֹנָי אֱלֹהֵינוּ מֶלֶךְ הָעוֹלָם אֲשֶׁר קִדְּשָׁנוּ בְּמִצְוֹתָיו
וְצִוָּנוּ עַל אֲכִלַת מָרוֹר.

*Ba-ruch Atah Adonai Elo-hei-nu Me-lech ha-Olam, ash-er
kid-sha-nu b'mits-vo-tav v'tsi-va-nu al a-chi-lat mah-ror.*

Blessed art Thou, O Lord our God, King
of the universe, who sanctified us with
His commandments, and commanded us
concerning the eating of the bitter herbs.

All eat together of the maror.

―――

KORECH, EATING OF THE BITTER HERBS AND *CHAROSET*

The *charoset* (sweet mixture) symbolizes the mortar the
children of Israel used to make the bricks as they toiled
under Pharaoh's harsh taskmasters. It is eaten with matzah.

In order to settle a controversy about how the Passover is to
be eaten, Rabbi Hillel, a famous sage, began the tradition of
the "Hillel sandwich," which is made by eating the maror
and the charoset together between two pieces of matzah. It
is also said that this combination of bitter and sweet reminds
us that God's promise can bring joy in the midst of sorrow.

Each person takes two small pieces of matzah and places some charoset and maror in the middle. All eat together.

BEITZAH, THE ROASTED EGG

The roasted egg on the Seder plate brings to mind the roasted daily Temple sacrifice that no longer can be offered because the Temple no longer stands. In the very midst of the Passover Seder, Jewish people are reminded that there is no sacrifice to bring righteousness before God. We take a piece of the egg and dip it in salt water, a symbol of tears, and all eat.

THIS CONCLUDES THE FIRST PORTION OF THE SEDER

SHULCHAN ORECH, THE SET TABLE

The Passover meal can now be served. Eat, tell stories, and enjoy! Be sure to use the recipes included in this book (see chapter 6, "Passover Foods and Recipes," by Mitch Forman).

TZAFUN, FINDING AND EATING THE AFIKOMAN

After the meal is finished, the leader of the Seder sends the children to find the afikoman, which is the middle piece of matzah that was broken, wrapped in a napkin and hidden before the meal. The child who finds it brings it to the leader of the Seder, who redeems the afikoman with a symbolic reward, usually some money or chocolate.

According to tradition, the leader of the Seder then unwraps the afikoman, blesses it, and breaks it up into small olive-sized pieces. He then distributes a small piece to everyone seated around the table and all eat the afikoman together.

For believers in Yeshua, there is great significance in this tradition. We believe that it was at this point in the Passover Seder when Yeshua seized the moment to reveal to His disciples His identity and the pending suffering and death that He would soon endure. The Gospel of Luke records Messiah's words on this occasion: *"And when He had taken some bread and given thanks, He broke it and gave it to them, saying, 'This is My body which is given for you; do this in remembrance of Me'"* (Luke 22:19).

We believe that Yeshua Himself was the middle piece of matzah, the piece representing the priest or mediator between God and the people. He was broken in death, wrapped for burial, and resurrected from the dead. The matzah represents His sin-free (unleavened) sacrifice for our redemption from sin and death.

When the leader of the Seder unwraps the afikoman and distributes a piece to everyone seated at the table, it reminds us that Yeshua the Messiah distributed His life to all who believe.

We might also reflect upon the appearance of traditional matzah, which is made both striped and pierced, as His body was striped and pierced (Isa. 53:5). This middle piece of matzah, the afikoman, is the "Bread of Life" (John 6:35) we share in the Lord's Supper or Communion as believers.

Having explained this to the participants, now the leader breaks the afikoman into olive-sized pieces and gives one to each person to hold briefly as together they reflect on the sacrifice that Yeshua endured in His body. Then all partake in unison after the following prayer is said:

בָּרוּךְ אַתָּה אֲדֹנָי אֱלֹהֵינוּ מֶלֶךְ הָעוֹלָם הַמּוֹצִיא לֶחֶם מִן הָאָרֶץ.

Ba-ruch Atah Adonai Elo-hei-nu Me-lech Ha-Olam,
Ha-mo-tzi le-chem min ha-ah-retz.

Blessed art Thou, O Lord our God, King of the
universe, who brings forth bread from the earth.

HA GEULAH, THIRD CUP: THE CUP OF REDEMPTION

The Cup of Redemption is based on God's promise in
Exodus 6:6, *"I will also redeem you with an outstretched arm
and with great judgments."* It is a reminder of the lamb's
blood, the price paid for Israel's promised redemption. In
the same way, Yeshua likely took this cup and spoke the
words in Luke 22:20, *"This cup which is poured out for you
is the new covenant in My blood."* In so doing, He spoke
of a greater redemption than the Israelites experienced
in Egypt. Yeshua had in mind the redemption and
deliverance of humankind, forgiven of sin through the
shed blood of the Lamb of God. Yeshua is quoting from
the great New Covenant prophecy given by the prophet
Jeremiah in Jeremiah 31:31–34.

The cup is filled and the following blessing is recited:

בָּרוּךְ אַתָּה אֲדֹנָי אֱלֹהֵינוּ מֶלֶךְ הָעוֹלָם בּוֹרֵא פְּרִי הַגָּפֶן.

Baruch Atah Adonai Elo-hei-nu Me-lech ha-Olam,
boh-ray pri ha-gah-fen.

Blessed art Thou, O Lord our God, King of the
universe, Creator of the fruit of the vine.

All drink leaning to the left.

ELIYAHU, ELIJAH'S CUP (LUKE 1:17; MALACHI 4:5–6)

The Bible tells us in Malachi 4:5 that Elijah will appear to
herald the coming of the Messianic King:

Behold, I am going to send you Elijah the prophet before the coming of the great and terrible day of the Lord.

It is tradition to have an additional place setting, complete with a cup of the fruit of the vine, for Elijah at Passover. The leader of the Seder usually sends a child to the front door to look outside and see if Elijah is coming. Thus far, he has never attended a Seder!

But has he? The Bible tells us in Luke 1:17, speaking of John the Baptist, *"It is he who will go as a forerunner before Him in the spirit and power of Elijah."* John did indeed come to fulfill Elijah's role as herald to announce the first coming of the Messiah, fulfilled in the coming of Yeshua.

HALLEL, FOURTH CUP: THE CUP OF PRAISE

What is the proper response to redemption? Joy, of course! We rejoice, knowing that the Jewish people were delivered from Egyptian bondage and that both Jewish and Gentile followers of the Messiah were redeemed from the bondage of sin and death. The fourth and final cup of the Passover Seder is the Cup of Praise—a cup of rejoicing, joy, and consummation. It is the first taste of freedom beyond redemption. It is a reminder of Israel's promised future beyond slavery in Egypt—dwelling instead in freedom in the Promised Land. In many ways, this cup also foreshadows the glorious future for Israel and the world to come in the age of the Messianic kingdom.

The cup is filled, all lift it and the following blessing is recited:

בָּרוּךְ אַתָּה אֲדֹנָי אֱלֹהֵינוּ מֶלֶךְ הָעוֹלָם בּוֹרֵא פְּרִי הַגָּפֶן.

Baruch Atah Adonai Elo-hei-nu Me-lech ha-Olam, boh-ray pri ha-gah-fen.

130

Blessed art Thou, O Lord our God, King of the
universe, Creator of the fruit of the vine.

All drink leaning to the left.

HALLEL PSALMS (PSALMS 113–18)

In the spirit of joy and celebration, we rejoice together
for all that God has done for us! He has set us apart to
be His people, He has brought us out of slavery, He has
redeemed us, and He has brought us to Himself. For all of
this we praise Him! As the Seder comes to a close we go
out singing the Hallel Psalms (Pss. 113–18). It is incredible
to realize that in Yeshua's last moments of freedom and
fellowship on earth, He and His disciples also sang as they
finished their Seder and went out to the Mount of Olives
(Matt. 26:30; Mark 14:26).

This is a wonderful opportunity to read and reflect on these
psalms together, and consider the strong Messianic under-
tones of each. There are traditional tunes for these songs, but
we also encourage you to find some traditional hymns or
contemporary worship songs that are based on these Psalms.

NEXT YEAR IN JERUSALEM!

It is tradition to conclude the Seder with a joyous procla-
mation of hope and faith by reciting in unison:

לְשָׁנָה הַבָּאָה בִּרוּשָׁלַיִם!

L'Shana HaBa'ah B'Yerushalayim!

"Next Year in Jerusalem!"

This has great meaning to followers of Jesus the Messiah
because we expect Him to return! We do not know the
day of His second coming, but we wait in hope knowing

that as surely as the Messiah came once to redeem us from sin, so He will come again as judge to establish His kingdom. As God promises through the prophet Isaiah,

> *For a child will be born to us, a son will be given to us;*
> *and the government will rest on His shoulders; and His*
> *name will be called Wonderful Counselor,*
> *Mighty God, Eternal Father, Prince of Peace.*
> *There will be no end to the increase of His government or*
> *of peace, on the throne of David and over his*
> *kingdom, to establish it and to uphold it with justice*
> *and righteousness from then on and forevermore.*
> *The zeal of the Lord of hosts will*
> *accomplish this.* (Isa. 9:6–7)

And as the Apostle Paul writes, in light of our expectation of Messiah's return,

> *Therefore, my beloved brethren, be steadfast, immovable,*
> *always abounding in the work of the Lord, knowing that*
> *your toil is not in vain in the Lord.* (1 Cor. 15:58)

Happy Passover!

6

Passover Foods and Recipes

MITCH FORMAN

The special foods we eat are a major part of the way we celebrate the Jewish holidays. In fact every feast has something to do with food except one, the Day of Atonement, in which Jewish people eat nothing at all. Passover is the culinary epitome of the entire year.

So why the connection between food and feasts? As a chef I can only answer this from my own experience. Everyone has to eat to sustain life. However, on occasion people will eat out at a special restaurant to celebrate a major event. Everyone remembers the one or two exceptional meals they have especially enjoyed, and often what they ate commemorating that day.

By connecting food to the feasts, we enter into a greater experience of the holy days as the ceremonies engage our sense of smell and taste, and the foods we eat help to create memories for a lifetime. In fact, there are three foods biblically mandated for Jewish people to eat on Passover. These are lamb, bitter herbs, and unleavened bread.

> *Your lamb shall be an unblemished male a year old; you*
> *may take it from the sheep or from the goats. You shall*

keep it until the fourteenth day of the same month, then
the whole assembly of the congregation of Israel is to kill
it at twilight. Moreover, they shall take some of the blood
and put it on the two doorposts and on the lintel of the
houses in which they eat it. They shall eat the flesh that
same night, roasted with fire, and they shall eat it with
unleavened bread and bitter herbs. (Exod. 12:5–8)

Jewish people still eat unleavened bread (matzah) and bitter herbs during the Passover Seder. However, certain groups of Jewish people no longer eat lamb at Passover in remembrance of the destruction of the Temple.

Before we continue on with various recipes, we need to distinguish between the two major groups of Jewish people in the world. Jewish people are often defined religiously as Orthodox, Conservative, or Reform. But the greater distinction has to do with where these groups of Jewish people come from and the traditions that have developed as a result of their differing backgrounds from where they live. The first major group is the Ashkenazic Jews, who trace their roots back to Germany and Eastern Europe. The second major group is the Sephardic Jews, who were originally from Spain, and today are mostly from Spain, Portugal, North Africa, and other parts of the Middle East.

Curiously, Sephardic Jews will eat lamb at Passover, but Ashkenazic Jews will not. Jewish people from Sephardic backgrounds also eat rice at Passover, which Ashkenazic Jews view as leavened. Rice and lamb are a more significant part of the overall diet for Jews from the Middle East and North Africa than for Jewish people from either Eastern or Western Europe, which may be one reason for these differences.

As you can easily see, Jewish people are not demographically monolithic, and therefore the foods attached to the various holidays differ quite a bit depending on where Jewish people have their roots. In Israel it is quite remarkable in that there is almost a 50/50 mix between Ashkenazic and Sephardic Jews and considerable intermarriage between them. Therefore, the eating of lamb might be even more common in Israel than it is in North America or Europe.

Some of my fondest memories of celebrating Passover were spent at my grandparents' homes. Both grandmothers would cook up a feast. As is no doubt true for most Jewish families, on Passover we eat foods that are both biblical and traditional, and over time these foods have become synonymous with the Passover Seder.

So now to those recipes! This chapter is divided into two sections. The first section will provide instructions and recipes for setting your Passover table using traditional Passover foods, and the second section will describe a traditional Passover dinner and show you how to prepare it. If you are not Jewish, then you might want to try the discipline of abstaining from foods made with leaven or yeast and see what your Jewish friends experience!

A TRADITIONAL SEDER MEAL

THE SEDER PLATE

The Seder plate is where the foods used during the Passover Seder are placed. This includes the **karpas** (parsley), **charoset** (apple mixture), **maror** (bitter herbs), **beitzah** (roasted egg), and **zeroah** (lamb shankbone). (Note pronunciations of key terms below and throughout this chapter.)

Preparing the Seder plate requires precision. The foods we eat on Passover are there by design and used during the service to enhance and embellish the story of God's redemption of the children of Israel from Egypt.

Although every home has its own traditions, most families follow the same basic pattern for the Seder. Passover, which includes the Festival of Unleavened Bread, is observed for eight days. The Seder is celebrated on the first night of the Feast, and on the second night as well outside of Israel. The second Seder traditionally has allowed for families outside of Israel to hold their Seder on the right night based upon the lunar calendar and timing detailed in Scripture,

> *In the first month, on the fourteenth day of the month at twilight is the* Lord's *Passover.* (Lev. 23:5)

The foods placed on the Seder plate are listed below, and we have explained the reason why each is included, the means of preparing it, and the role the food plays in the Passover Seder. Ordinarily, each person will have a Seder plate with the following foods.

Maror (mah-ROAR)

The bitter herb, usually horseradish, again represents the bitterness of life for slaves in Egypt.

Preparation: Freshly grated horseradish can be used, or you may choose to buy a jar of prepared horseradish. Provide one tablespoon for every eight persons at the Seder. (Note: Simply be aware that this amount of horseradish is strong enough to make most people shed tears, especially children.)

Role in the Seder: We eat bitter herbs as commanded in Scripture. It causes us to cry (or at least shed tears) as we remember that our people cried out to God because of the bitterness of their lives as slaves in Egypt.

Karpas (CAR-pahs)

A green vegetable, usually parsley, signifying springtime. It also reminds us of the hyssop (herbaceous plant) that was used by the Israelites to apply the blood to the doors of their homes.

Preparation: Clean a bunch of parsley, rinse and dry. Set out one spring for each person present.

Role in the Seder: This is the first item eaten in the Seder. We dip the parsley into salt water, which symbolizes tears, to remind us that life in bondage produces tears.

Charoset (khah-ROH-set)

A sweet apple mixture made with dates, nuts, and honey that is left standing out for a time to turn brown. This symbolizes the mortar used in Egypt for making bricks.

Preparation:

Ingredients:

4 red apples	½ cup sweet red wine
1 cup chopped walnuts	or grape juice
½ cup chopped dates	½ teaspoon cinnamon
¼ cup of honey	¼ teaspoon nutmeg

Instructions:
1. Peel and grate the apple.
2. Mix in the nuts, dates, honey and spices.
3. Add the wine and mix well.
4. Refrigerate until serving. The mixture will turn brown.

Yield: 12 portions

Role in the Seder: The charoset represents our labor in Egypt and the sweetness of the mixture gives us hope for the promise of redemption.

BEITZAH (BAY-TZAH)

A roasted egg symbolizing the annual sacrifices (called the *hagigah*) that are no longer offered in the Temple.

Preparation: Roast one egg for the Seder plate and roast additional eggs, one per every four people. This should take about 1 hour at 350°F in the oven to roast. Many Jewish people simply use a brown egg or actually boil it in coffee to give the egg a roasted appearance.

Part in the Seder: Place one roasted egg, which has turned brown in the oven, on the Seder plate. The additional eggs are peeled and sliced and will be eaten right before the meal. This browned appearance is important as the egg is supposed to remind us of the missing sacrifices that were roasted on the altar at the Temple.

ZEROAH (ZEH-ROH-AH)

The shankbone of a lamb reminds us of the Passover lamb. The first Passover lambs were sacrificed at twilight, and their blood was smeared on the doorposts and lintel of the Israelite homes.

Preparation: The shankbone of a leg of lamb is roasted on high heat until browned.

Role in the Seder: The shankbone reminds us of the lamb that was sacrificed at the first Passover in Egypt and in ensuing days in the Temple.

SALT WATER

Used to symbolize the tears of life. Serves as a dip for both the *karpas* and the *beitzah*.

THE MATZAH TASH

Matzah is the unleavened bread described as the bread of affliction. During Passover we do not eat foods that contain leaven. It is one of the most important symbols on the Passover table. We have a special pouch called a *matzah tash* (MAHTZ-uh TAHSH) in which we place three pieces of matzah.

Our Jewish tradition allows for variety of opinion on the meaning of the three sections, but one pouch. Some say it represents the priesthood of Judaism: the priests, the Levites, and the people of Israel. Others say it represents the three Patriarchs: Abraham, Isaac, and Jacob. Still others say it represents the three cakes Abraham served to the angels who visited him. Some Messianic Jews take this a step further and view the three pieces, yet one pouch of the matzah tash as representing the tri-unity of God: the Father, the Son, and the Holy Spirit.

THE FRUIT OF THE VINE

The wine at Passover is always red, representing the blood of the lamb. Jewish people usually use a sweet red kosher wine made by companies such as Manischewitz, Mogen David, and Kedem. Kosher grape juice for children and adults who do not drink wine is always acceptable. Everyone drinks four cups of the fruit of the vine at the Seder. Traditionally, the four cups represent the four statements on redemption found in Exodus 6:6–7:

Say, therefore, to the sons of Israel, "I am the LORD, and I will bring you out from under the burdens of the Egyptians, and I will deliver you from their bondage. I will also redeem you with an outstretched arm and with great judgments. Then I will take you for My people, and I will be your God; and you shall know that I am the LORD your God, who brought you out from under the burdens of the Egyptians."

The four cups representing these four statements on redemption are also named as follows:

1. The Cup of Sanctification (or Blessing):
   "I will bring you out from under the burdens of the Egyptians" (v. 6).

2. The Cup of Plagues (or Judgment):
   "I will deliver you from their bondage" (v. 6).

3. The Cup of Redemption:
   "I will also redeem you with an outstretched arm" (v. 6).

4. The Cup of Praise (or Rejoicing):
   "I will take you for My people" (v. 7).

PASSOVER SEDER DINNER RECIPES

Matzah Ball Soup

This soup, favored by the Ashkenazic Jews, is made from a mixture of matzah meal and chicken fat and is the traditional soup served on Passover. We all know that it was our grandmother who made the best matzah ball soup, so no two recipes are the same, except that the standard soup includes chicken soup and matzah balls. In some Jewish homes, soft noodles will be added to the soup, along with carrots and sometimes celery, etc.

Ingredients:

For the Matzah Balls:

4 eggs
2 tablespoons chicken
   fat (substitute oil if
   you can't find fat)
½ teaspoon salt

2 tablespoons soup stock
   or water
1 cup matzah meal (buy
   it at the store)

Instructions:
1. Beat eggs slightly with fork in a bowl.
2. Add chicken fat, salt, and water.
3. Add matzah meal gradually until it thickens.
4. Refrigerate for 20 minutes in a covered bowl.
   This will allow the matzah to absorb the liquid
   and make it easier to use.
5. Scoop out portions of the matzah ball mixture
   with a standard ice cream scoop and with wet
   hands, form into balls.
6. Fill a medium-sized stock pot half way with water
   and bring to simmer on medium heat.
7. Cook for 30 minutes.
8. Drain and set aside.

Yield: 16 matzah balls

Ingredients:

For the Chicken Soup:

1 chicken (5 pounds),
   quartered
2 medium size onions,
   diced

6 carrots, diced
1 stalk celery, diced
water to cover
2 tablespoons salt

Instructions:
1. Peel onions and carrots and wash celery and cut
   all vegetables into ½-inch cubes.
2. Place chicken and vegetables in large stock pot.

3. Add salt and water to cover.
4. Bring to boil and then lower the flame and simmer for 2 hours.
5. Remove chicken parts and let cool. Remove the chicken meat from the bones and shred.
6. Strain the soup of all the vegetables pieces and bring chicken stock back to a simmer.
7. Add the shredded chicken to soup and keep on a low simmer.
8. About 30 minutes before serving, add the matzah balls to the soup and simmer.
9. Dish out soup with 1 matzah ball per serving.

Yield: 14 to 16 servings

Gefilte Fish

Gefilte fish is a prized delicacy for Jewish people who come from Eastern Europe, where using every part of the fish was necessary for life when one had very little to eat. The term *gefilte* (guh-FILL-teh) is Yiddish for "stuffed fish." It bears a resemblance to fish pâté that is eaten cold. Jewish people love eating this on Shabbat dinners and festival meals.

Since gefilte fish is an acquired taste, we recommend that you buy a jar of gefilte fish in the Jewish section of the supermarket to try it first. It is traditionally served with horseradish. However, for those of you who are more adventurous, you may try to make your own. This recipe comes from a friend's mom who, legend has it, made gefilte fish that was out of this world!

For the gefilte fish balls:

3 pounds whitefish★	2 medium carrots
3 pounds carp★	1 celery stalk
3 medium onions	3 large eggs

2 teaspoons sugar   ½ cup matzah meal
1 teaspoons salt   ½ cup cold water
½ teaspoon pepper   1 jar of red or white
¾ cup corn oil   prepared horseradish

*Go to your local fish market and ask for these fish to be skinned and filleted. Ask the fish dealer to give you the heads and bones as well for the stock. Note that you may need to order ahead for whole fish.

Instructions:

1. In a food processor grind the fish until very smooth. (You may also put the fish in an electric mixer and macerate with a dough hook. However, the onions and carrots will still need to be ground in a food processor before adding to the fish mixture.)

2. Then add 2 onions and 1 carrot and grind until smooth. (You may have to make this in two batches if your food processor cannot hold all the ingredients.)

3. Take the fish mixture and in a large bowl add the water a little at a time until all the water is incorporated into the mixture.

4. Then add the eggs, sugar, salt, pepper, and mix very well with a wooden spoon.

5. Stir in the matzah meal, and mix until everything is incorporated.

6. Refrigerate overnight in a covered container.

7. The next day, place the fish bones and heads in a stock pot with 1 onion, 1 carrot, and celery stalk, all diced. Fill the stock pot halfway with water and bring to a boil and then lower to simmer for 1½ hours.

8. Next remove the fish mixture from the refrigerator to make fish patties. (To make patties

take some of the fish mixture and place in a big metal spoon and then slowly drop the fish ball in the simmering fish stock.

9. Cook the fish patties for 1½ hours.
10. Remove fish patties, onions, and carrots from the stock pot and place on a paper towel to dry and cool.
11. Place the fish patties with the onions and carrot in a closed container and place in the refrigerator overnight.
12. Place 2 pieces of gefilte fish with some onions and carrots pieces on a plate and eat with red or white horseradish.

Yield: 12 patties (4-ounce portions)

Chopped Liver

Chopped liver is part of most Jewish people's upbringing. My two grandmothers made their chopped liver a little differently from each other, but both were tasty. This recipe combines the best of each. Chopped liver is a developed taste, but to get the full Jewish experience at Passover, we recommend you at least try a little bit on a piece of matzah.

Ingredients:
1½ pounds chicken livers, trimmed
3 eggs
1 large onion, sliced
2 tablespoons chicken schmaltz[16]
    (or 2 tablespoons olive oil)
2 tablespoons Passover wine or chicken stock
salt and freshly ground black pepper to taste

16 Chicken schmaltz (SHMALTZ) is rendered chicken fat.

Instructions:

1. Hard-boil the eggs for 10 minutes, drain, and set aside.

2. In a sauté pan, cook the onions on low heat until a nice golden brown color appears. Remove from the pan and let cool on a paper towel.

3. Add wine and chicken schmaltz to the sauté pan and bring to simmer on medium heat.

4. Add the livers and cook for 5 minutes or until the livers are firm to the touch.

5. Pour mixture into a food processor and mix until the ingredients come together, but not too smooth.

6. Scrape mixture into a bowl.

7. Grate the eggs and add to the bowl. Then add the onions and mix together.

8. Salt and pepper to taste.

9. Refrigerate overnight and serve the next day.

To make chicken schmaltz:

1. Take the spare fat from a raw chicken. This can be done by removing the skin and fat from chicken thighs and cutting into strips.

2. Cook on low heat in a sauté pan with 2 sticks (8 ounces) of butter for 60 to 90 minutes until all fat has been rendered gently out of the chicken skin.

3. Remove skin from pan and drain on paper towels to form *gribenes* (Yiddish for "cracklings").

4. Pour the fat (schmaltz[17]) into a bowl and refrigerate until needed.

---

17 The schmaltz (fat) will keep for up to 3 to 4 weeks in the fridge if stored correctly with a lid.

Tzimmes

Tzimmes (TSIM-ess) is one of those Jewish dishes that doesn't sound good when reading the ingredients, but one taste of this gooey, sticky, roasted vegetable dish will have you wanting more! The sweetness of this dish reminds us of the sweetness of redemption.

Ingredients:

8 ounces apple juice
1 cup honey
2 teaspoons salt
1 teaspoon pepper
2 teaspoons tarragon
8 carrots, chopped

2 yellow onions, chopped
2 turnips, chopped
4 sweet potatoes, peeled and diced
8 ounces dried apricots, chopped

Instructions:

1. Preheat oven to 350°F.
2. Heat the apple juice, honey, salt, pepper, and tarragon and simmer in a small pot.
3. Place the vegetables and apricots in a 4-inch casserole dish.
4. Pour the honey and juice mixture over the vegetable/apricot mixture.
5. Cover and cook in oven at 350°F for 90 minutes.
6. Remove cover and cook for 30 minutes more, and serve.

Yield: 10 to 12 servings

Egg Noodle Kugel

Noodle kugel (COO-gull) is a casserole of noodles drenched in an egg mixture. It is made with egg noodles, so it is kosher for Passover. When it is done, you will be introduced to a savory meal that has sweetness to it as well.

Ingredients:

1 package (16-ounce) wide egg noodles	8 ounces raisins
6 large eggs	½ cup sugar
1 pound sour cream	1 stick (8 ounces) unsalted butter, melted
8 ounces cottage cheese	¼ teaspoon salt
8 ounces cream cheese, softened	4 tablespoons cinnamon
	4 tablespoons nutmeg

Instructions:

1. Preheat oven to 350°F.
2. Add the noodles to a pot of boiling water and cook for 5 minutes, or until soft.
3. In a food processor combine the eggs, sour cream, cottage cheese, and cream cheese and mix until smooth.
4. Add sugar, melted butter, and salt and blend well.
5. Place noodles mixed with raisins in a 9 x 13-inch glass baking dish and pour egg mixture over noodles.
6. Sprinkle mixture with cinnamon and nutmeg.
7. Cover dish with aluminum foil and bake for 60 minutes.
8. Remove from oven and let sit for 15 minutes.
9. Cut into squares and serve warm.

Yield: 10 to 12 servings

Roast Brisket

Brisket is always a favorite at Passover season. In fact my family would always prepare a roast brisket for the Passover Seder. Here is the recipe my grandma used, my mom used, and now I use.

Ingredients:

1 whole beef brisket (8 pounds)
10 cloves garlic, peeled and smashed
2 yellow onions, sliced
6 carrots, sliced
32 ounces tomato puree
2 cups beef stock
salt and pepper to taste

Instructions:

1. Preheat oven to 350°F.
2. Heat a sauté pan on high for 2 minutes and sear the brisket on each side for 3 minutes.
3. Place sliced onions and carrots on the bottom of a large roasting pan and set the brisket on top with the fat side up.
4. Coat the brisket with the smashed garlic, tomato puree, and salt and pepper to taste. Then add the beef stock.
5. Cover pan and cook the brisket for 3 hours at 350°F.
6. When meat is done, remove from pan and let sit for 30 minutes.
7. Slice the meat against the grain in ¼-inch slices and serve with the onions and carrots.
8. Reduce remaining tomato broth till thick and pour over the meat, and serve.

Yield: 12 to 16 servings

Macaroons

Macaroons are made every Passover season. They are unleavened and the egg whites mixed with the coconut binds the cookie together. This recipe allows the sugar to spread to the edges and caramelize. These cookies are so easy to make, yet they taste so good. For a variation, add the cocoa powder to the mixture and make chocolate macaroons.

Ingredients:

1 package (14-ounce) sweetened shredded coconut

4 large egg whites, beaten

1 tablespoon grated orange zest

½ cup sugar

1 tablespoon grated lemon zest

¼ teaspoon salt

½ cup cocoa powder (optional)

Instructions:
1. Preheat oven to 340°F.
2. Line a baking sheet with parchment paper.
3. Combine the coconut, sugar, orange and lemon zest, and salt.
4. Beat the egg whites and add to the coconut mixture.
5. Place heaping tablespoons of the mixture on the parchment-lined baking sheet, spacing the mixture 3 wide by 4 long for 12 macaroons per sheet.
6. Cook the macaroons for about 20 minutes or until the edges start turning brown.
7. Cool on a wire rack for 30 minutes and serve.

Yield: 12 macaroons (2-ounce cookies)

Enjoy!!

CONCLUSION:
Messiah in Your Passover

DARRELL L. BOCK AND
MITCH GLASER

Whereas it is our hope that both Jewish and Gentile
seekers will read this book, *The Gospel in the Passover*,
we understand that the majority of readers will already
be followers of Jesus the Messiah. Knowing this, the
book was designed to deepen the Bible knowledge
and discipleship of those who have come to know
the glorious truths of salvation through the Lamb of
God—Jesus the Messiah—while also being accessible to
everyone.

I know we speak on behalf of our authors with the hope
that you will be blessed, and have a better understanding
of the following:

1. The Jewish context of the New Testament.

2. The Jewish heritage of the Messiah Himself.

3. The significance of the Passover throughout
   Scripture.

4. The ways in which Jewish people observe the
   Passover.

5. The Jewish roots of our faith in Yeshua the Messiah.

6. The ways in which Jewish people interpret the Bible.

7. How to share the Gospel with Jewish people through the Passover in a more knowledgeable and sensitive manner.

8. The links between the Last Supper and the Lord's Supper.

9. Redemption and the shadow of salvation, which the Exodus and Passover events cast upon all of Scripture and Jewish life.

10. How to have a deeper love for the God of Israel, the people of Israel, and the Messiah of Israel.

11. How to celebrate Messiah in the Passover in our own homes and churches.

12. What it means for Jesus to be the Lamb of God who takes away the sin of the world.

Thank you for taking the time to read this book. We pray that it will continue to impact your life for many years and many Passovers to come. Most of all, we hope that by joining us in this pilgrimage you will now have a better understanding of our glorious Jewish Messiah and Savior—Jesus, *Yeshua*—the Lamb of God who not only takes away the sins of the world, but because of His mercy and grace has removed our sins *"as far as the east is from the west"* (Ps. 103:12).

We hope the Lord will use this new understanding of the Gospel in the Passover to deepen your walk of faith until He comes again!

SCRIPTURE INDEX

Topical Index

ABOUT THE GENERAL EDITORS

Darrell L. Bock is Executive Director of Cultural Engagement and Senior Research Professor of New Testament Studies, Dallas Theological Seminary. He has earned recognition as a Humboldt Scholar (Tübingen University in Germany) and as author of over forty books, including well regarded commentaries on Luke and Acts, studies of the historical Jesus, and work in cultural engagement as host of the Seminary's Table Podcasts (www.dts.edu/thetable). He was president of the Evangelical Theological Society (ETS) for 2000–2001, is a consulting editor for *Christianity Today*, and serves on the boards of Wheaton College and Chosen People Ministries. His articles appear in leading publications, and he often is an expert for the media on New Testament issues. He has been a *New York Times* best-selling author in nonfiction and is elder emeritus at Trinity Fellowship Church in Dallas. When traveling overseas, he will tune into the current game involving his favorite teams from Houston—live—even in the wee hours of the morning. He and his wife Sally are proud parents of two daughters and a son and are also grandparents.

Mitch Glaser is the President of Chosen People Ministries in New York City. He has been extensively involved in Jewish evangelism in several countries and was instrumental in helping to establish a congregation among Russian Jewish immigrants in New York. He is the corecipient of *Christianity Today*'s Award of Merit in the Apologetics/Evangelism category for 2009 for the book *To the Jew First: The Case for Jewish Evangelism in Scripture and History*, coedited with Darrell L. Bock. He is also the coauthor of *The Fall Feasts of Israel* and has written many articles for Christian periodicals and has taught at leading evangelical schools such as Fuller Theological Seminary and Moody Bible Institute. Mitch earned a Master of Divinity degree in Old Testament Studies at the Talbot School of Theology and a Doctor of Philosophy in Intercultural Studies at Fuller Theological Seminary. Mitch and his wife have two daughters.